WOOD PLANK PROJECTS

WOOD PLANK PROJECTS

30 Simple and Creative DIY Décor Ideas for Your Home and Garden

CARRIE SPALDING

Skyhorse Publishing

Skyhorse Publishing books may be purchased in bulk at special discounts for sales promotion, corporate gifts, fund-raising, or educational purposes. Special editions can also be created to specifications. For details, contact the Special Sales Department, Skyhorse Publishing, 307 West 36th Street, 11th Floor, New York, NY 10018 or info@skyhorsepublishing.com.

Skyhorse® and Skyhorse Publishing® are registered trademarks of Skyhorse Publishing, Inc.®, a Delaware corporation.

Visit our website at www.skyhorsepublishing.com.

10 9 8 7 6 5 4 3

Library of Congress Cataloging-in-Publication Data is available on file.

Cover design by Qualcom
Cover photo credit: Carrie Spalding

Print ISBN: 978-1-5107-4294-9
Ebook ISBN: 978-1-5107-4295-6

Printed in China

For Mitch. For believing in me so hard,
I can't help believing in me, too.

Table of Contents

INTRODUCTION   **ix**

MATERIALS AND TOOLS   **1**

WOODEN SIGNS   **11**

Simple Framed Sign   **13**

Stenciled Wooden Clipboard   **17**

Reclaimed Wood Sign   **21**

Wood Plank Photo Board   **27**

Rustic Pallet Wood Sign   **33**

United States Outline Sign   **37**

WALL DÉCOR   **41**

Rustic Barnwood Frame   **43**

Scrap Wood Sunburst Mirror   **47**

Weathered Wall Vase Hangers   **51**

Reclaimed Wood Wreath   **55**

Rustic Barnwood Quilt   **59**

Oversized Farmhouse Clock   **65**

HOME DÉCOR   **73**

Herb Garden Planter Box   **75**

Vintage Doorknob Wall Hooks   **79**

Colorful Wooden Bunting   **83**

Wooden Boot Tray   **87**

Wooden Arrow Growth Chart   **91**

Reclaimed Wood Shelves   **95**

OUTDOOR DÉCOR   99

Address Sign with Planter   **101**

Simple Outdoor Wood Lanterns   **105**

Vertical Wall Planter   **109**

Shaker-Style Wood Shutters   **113**

Wooden Planter Box   **117**

Indoor/Outdoor X Bench   **123**

STATEMENT-MAKING PIECES   129

Weathered Wood Plank Wall   **131**

Curvy Wooden Headboard   **137**

Farmhouse Bench   **143**

Removable Herringbone Tabletop   **149**

Reclaimed Wood Barn Door   **155**

Rustic Farmhouse Dining Table   **161**

EPILOGUE: You Can Do This!   169

Introduction

When I think about woodworking, a very specific image comes to mind. I picture an older man with a big, fluffy beard tucked away in a workshop that is filled with every tool imaginable, where he creates intricately turned table legs and joins beautiful bits of wood by hand. It's a cozy image, and I'm sure there are woodworkers out there who fit the stereotype—but many do not.

I certainly don't. I'm a suburban mom of three little boys, and my workshop is a space in the corner of our basement with only the most basic power tools and far too many spiders. Yet, I am definitely a woodworker. That's certainly not something I ever imagined I would call myself, but the truth is you don't have to be a master carpenter to be a woodworker; you just have to work with wood.

Many creative people talk about how they have always loved to make things since they were very young, and how their parents

always knew they would be an artist. Neither of these is true for me. I didn't consider myself particularly artistic, and I learned absolutely zero DIY skills growing up. But then I found myself the proud homeowner of a rundown brick ranch, and I wanted so badly to make it my own without spending a ton of money. My husband is a wonderful partner, but he isn't particularly handy or interested in spending his free time doing house projects, so it was up to me.

Slowly, I started learning how to do things myself, and I soon fell in love with the idea that I had the power to make things.

There is something magical about creating something with your own two hands. Instead of hoping and praying to find the exact item I wanted in stores, I could just design and make my own things in any style, size, and color I wanted.

The beautiful thing about working with wood is it really doesn't have to be complicated. Sure, there are absolutely amazing things that can be done with wood by people who are highly skilled. But there are also a lot of beautiful items that can be made by anyone who is willing to give it a try. Even better, you really don't have to have a lot of special

knowledge to get started with woodworking. You just need the desire. Once you know the basics of working with wood, you can create pretty much anything you could ever want.

Wood is almost magical—it is a strong and sturdy material that can be easily cut into any shape and size. It isn't all that expensive, and it can be given any finishing look you want. Wood manages to be both rustic and refined, strong and malleable—all at the same time. It is beautiful left untouched, and it is beautiful covered in layers of paint and stain. Wood can become a piece of furniture, or a simple sign, or even a house. Wood is gorgeous even when it is rustic and aged. In fact, I would argue that it actually becomes more attractive when it is decidedly "imperfect."

This book is filled with wooden décor projects that embrace the warmth, texture, and all of the glorious imperfections of wood. Many of these projects don't require special skills and can easily be completed in an afternoon. All of these projects use the most inexpensive wood planks available to make lovely décor pieces that will work with many different styles. Even if you have never considered yourself a woodworker—or a DIYer, for that matter—you can do this!

If you don't have much experience using tools and working with wood, start with a couple of easy projects to build your confidence. And if you are ready to just dive right into something more complicated, go for it. My hope is that you will be inspired to take these ideas and make them your own, customizing them with your own colors and finishes and touches. I hope you will come away from this book with the confidence that you, too, are a woodworker.

Materials and Tools

Here, I will walk you through the basics you need to know before diving into the projects in this book. You will learn about inexpensive lumber choices, reclaimed wood and where to find it, how to make new wood look old, paint and stain finishes, and the tools you will need.

Types of Wood Planks

Wood is such a versatile material, and there are many varieties. Each of the projects in this book name a specific type of wood you can use to complete them, but that is just a suggestion. Almost any project here can be made with a wide range of different types of wood.

Wood can be expensive, but it certainly doesn't have to be. In fact, sometimes the most humble, inexpensive types of wood give the most beautiful results.

Here are a few inexpensive wood plank choices that would work well for this book:

Furring strips are very roughly cut wood planks that builders use for leveling walls and making space for insulation. They are extremely inexpensive and work brilliantly when you want a more rustic wood plank but can't find reclaimed wood. Furring strips typically come in 1" x 2", 1" x 3", 1" x 4", and 2" x 2" planks.

Cedar fence pickets are a great wood choice for outdoor projects, since cedar naturally resists rot and decay. They are relatively inexpensive and can typically be found in the garden section of home improvement stores. They usually come in 1" x 6" x 6' planks.

Common board refers to less-expensive, lower-quality hardwood boards. The exact type of wood depends on what is most readily available at the time, but it is typically made from spruce, pine, or fir wood. This wood usually has more knotholes and imperfections than more expensive hardwoods, but it is much smoother and more uniform than furring strips. Common board comes is a huge range of widths and works very well for general DIY projects.

Plywood is not technically a wood plank, but it can easily be cut into strips that mimic planks. Plywood is less expensive than solid wood planks, and it works perfectly when you need a thinner or very lightweight piece of wood.

The Beauty of Reclaimed Wood

When you hear the term *reclaimed wood*, you might picture a stack of wide, weathered boards pulled from the sides of a historic barn from the 1800s. If you are ever lucky enough to find wood like that at a reasonable price, snatch it up! For the rest of us, luckily, reclaimed wood doesn't have to be barnwood—and it doesn't even have to be old.

Reclaimed wood is really just a fancy term for any wood that has been used before. The wood has already served a purpose, and now, instead of tossing it, you are giving it a new function.

I love to find old boards that show the rough saw marks from when they were milled, but I've also found plenty of beautiful wood to use right in my own scrap wood pile. Reclaimed wood is all about interesting textures and finishes, so look for anything that has previously been stained or painted, has lots of knotholes and texture, has been used outside and weathered, or even has paint drips from other projects.

Some examples of reclaimed wood

- Pallet wood
- Old fence boards
- Decking boards
- Old wood trim

- Old bed slats
- Pieces of broken wood furniture
- Wood from anything that has been taken apart

Where to Find Reclaimed Wood

Finding great wood to work with isn't nearly as hard as it seems. There are many easy places to find beautiful wood for projects that are usually very inexpensive or even free.

First, check your own basement, garage, shed, etc. If you're like most people, you've probably

stored all kinds of scraps and pieces away. These may not exactly be what you picture when you think of reclaimed wood, but remember: Something that looks like literal trash when piled in a shed can actually become really beautiful after it is cleaned up and given a purpose.

Ask your friends and family. Whenever I ask my family if anyone has scrap wood I can use for my projects, they always find all kinds of gorgeous wood for me in their own garages.

Look on the side of the road. Seriously, lots of people dump old pieces of wood from renovations or cleaned-out storage areas on the side of the road that are free for the taking. Just be sure to wear gloves if you pick them up.

Look on Craigslist, Facebook Marketplace, and other used marketplaces. There are always many people trying to get rid of old wood for free or for a fair price because they just want it out of their basements.

If all else fails, there are always pallets. There are always plenty of companies happy to get rid of old pallets. Pallets are easily broken down into wood planks that are full of texture and interest.

Working with Reclaimed Wood

Working with reclaimed wood is a bit different from working with freshly milled lumber from your local store. When choosing wood for your projects, look for wood planks that are straight and not twisted or warped. You also want to make sure the wood still feels strong and has not become brittle or rotten.

It is important to be aware that not all reclaimed wood is safe to work with. Some wood might have been treated with harsh chemicals or pesticides. Other wood may be harboring insects or may be full of rusty nails and other potential hazards. Be very careful when choosing your wood—and always wear gloves when handling it. Inspect the wood carefully for any signs of insects, mold, or discoloration. It helps if you have an idea of how the wood was previously used, which can give you clues as to whether it was likely treated with chemicals or insecticides. Wood that has been used in direct contact with the ground is generally not good for repurposing.

Many pallets in particular may have been treated with chemicals. When choosing a pallet, look for a clean pallet with no obvious spills. Pallets with no markings or labels are more likely to be safe to use, but always take care if using pallet wood for interior home projects. It is very important to be careful to avoid harmful woods. No project, no matter how creative, is ever worth your health.

Along the same lines, if you are working with old wood that has been previously painted, beware of lead paint. Many paints used before the 1970s contained high levels of lead. If you are working with any old painted wood, it is a good idea to do a simple lead test before cutting, sanding, or handling the wood.

It is important to clean all reclaimed wood well. Hose it down before bringing it into your workspace; then use a brush and the cleaner of your choice to scrub down each surface. If you have a lot of wood that needs to be cleaned, another option is to use a pressure washer to speed up cleaning time. Whatever method you choose, you will probably be surprised at just how much dirt and grime you clean off. The wood may even end up being a different color than you originally thought!

Making New Wood Look Old

There may be times when, no matter how open-minded you are, you really just can't find beautiful old wood to work with. In those pinches, there are several ways to get the same rustic, aged look when using brand-new wood.

If you are trying to mimic the vintage texture of reclaimed wood, start by choosing wood with plenty of imperfections. You still want to choose straight boards, but look for wood with a rougher texture. Knotholes, saw marks, and pronounced wood grain are all good things. Typically, inexpensive furring strips are perfect for when you want to make brand-new wood look aged. Fence pickets, which are also inexpensive, will work as well.

You can further rough up your wood in many different ways. Some options are hitting the wood with chains, pounding it with a hammer, scraping screws across the surface, and adding nail holes. All of these add roughness and signs of wear to the wood. If your wood already has pretty good texture, you can skip this step.

Once everything is nice and roughed up, you will want to lightly sand the edges and corners. Those crisp corners always get worn down with time and use, so sanding them will help mimic age. You can also sand off splinters, but be careful not to do too much sanding. After spending time choosing the perfect wood, you don't want to sand away all those beautiful imperfections. When you stain your wood, the stain will gather in these uneven areas and really highlight the texture.

Beautiful Wood Finishes

When it is time to finish your project, there are many, many different finishes and products you can use. Each technique will give a slightly different look, depending on the aesthetic you want.

Most of the projects here celebrate the beauty of the wood and choose either a stain or a weathered paint finish.

Stain. Basic wood stain has been used for hundreds of years because it is simple and beautiful. Stain is easy to apply, and there are many beautiful shades of stain to choose from. Different colors of stain can also be layered or mixed to create new shades. Stain can be applied using a clean rag or a paintbrush; always read the directions on your specific product to determine the best method before beginning.

Paint. Paint is extremely versatile. Using different techniques with paint, you can achieve all kinds of finishes.

- *Dry-brushing*: this is one of the easiest and simplest ways to use paint to get a weathered finish. Chip brushes are ideal for this, but you can also use any paintbrush. Put a very small amount of paint on your brush, and then wipe as much off on the lip of the paint can as possible. To remove even more paint, you can wipe your brush on a paper towel several times. Basically, you want your brush as dry as possible, while still having a bit of paint on it. Then, lightly brush your paint across your board. Because dry-brushing applies very little paint, you can add multiple colors without having to wait for the paint to dry in between.

- *Color washing*: You can also thin paint with water to create a semitransparent color wash. Wipe the paint over an existing finish to add a hint of color or lighten the previous finish.

- Another fun technique is to apply paint with a putty knife rather than a paintbrush. Load a small amount of paint on the end of the putty knife and quickly scrape it over the wood. Some areas will receive a lot of paint while others will remain unpainted. This technique is a great way to mimic aged, chippy paint finishes.

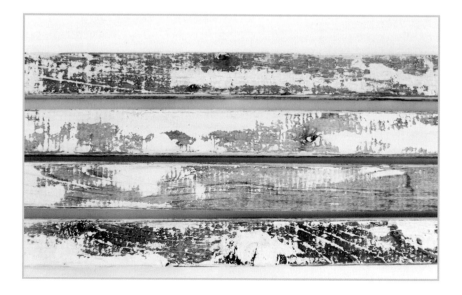

Paint and Stain Combos. Using a combination of stain and paint is another great method to achieve a beautiful, weathered finish. There are a few different ways to do this.

- Stain a piece first. Apply whatever stain you prefer and allow it to fully dry. Then, apply the paint of your choice. Once the paint has fully dried, you can use a high-grit sandpaper to distress the paint and reveal the dark wood beneath. The downside of this method is you have to be very careful not to sand right through the layer of stain as well.

- Apply paint to the wood first, by either dry-brushing the paint, applying it roughly with a putty knife, or painting a quick coat of paint and sanding some off. Follow this with a coat of wood stain. Immediately, go back over the wood with a clean rag dipped in mineral spirits. This will take most of the stain off the paint, while leaving the stain on any bits of bare wood that are peeking through.

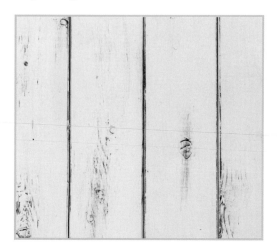

Sealer. Whether you choose to finish your project with paint or stain, you need to top it off with a good sealer. This will protect your piece and prevent the paint or stain from becoming worn and damaged. There are many kinds of sealers, or topcoats, available, including water-based and oil-based sealers in matte, satin, and gloss finishes. Always be sure to read the instructions on the specific sealer you choose to determine how it is best applied.

Tools You Will Need

All of the projects in this book are meant to be approachable for any DIYer. There aren't a lot of special tools used, and you probably already own most of the tools mentioned. Many projects only require a hammer, drill, or basic saw, but other projects do require a few power tools. If there are tools listed that you don't already own, they can easily be found at any home improvement store. If you aren't ready to commit to buying new tools, you can ask around to see if a friend has something you can borrow. Another option is to look for used tools on Craigslist, Facebook Marketplace, or at estate sales, where many used tools are available for great prices—this is how I bought most of my own power tools.

> ## Important!
> Always read the owner's manual before operating any power tool. Be sure to follow all instructions and safety precautions, including wearing protective eyewear at all times.

Saws. Most projects require some sort of saw. Usually, I don't specify the type of saw because multiple saws work well for cutting planks of wood to size. However, here is a list of specific saws you may need:

- A *miter saw* is a must for making any kind of angled cut. These also work well for making quick straight cuts on wood planks.

- A *jigsaw* works great for cutting curves and other unique shapes in wood. They are also good for making very small cuts.

- A *table saw* is good for ripping plywood and other large boards down to smaller sizes. If you don't have a table saw, you can probably have large pieces of wood cut down at the store at the time of purchase.

- A *circular saw* is handy for cutting straight lines in all types of wood.

Other power tools: Here are a few power tools that are needed for some projects.

- A *drill* is an essential for pretty much any DIY project. You will need it to drill holes, and it is also a much faster way for you to drive large numbers of screws into wood than a basic screwdriver.

- A *sander* is not a necessity, but it definitely makes any sanding job much faster.

- A *nail gun* is handy to have sometimes, though not essential. A hammer can do anything a nail gun can do; it just takes more time and energy.

- A *pocket hole jig* is a special tool that helps drill angled holes called pocket holes. This helps to make very strong joints for building furniture and other projects. There are several different pocket hole jigs available; if you don't already own one, I recommend starting out with one of the less expensive versions.

Project Difficulty

The projects in this book span a wide range of skill levels, from beginner to more advanced. Each project is labeled as "beginner," "easy," "moderate," or "advanced" so you can find projects that are a good fit for your skill level.

Beginner: You've got this, no problem. Even if you've never built anything before, you'll be fine.

Easy: These projects involve a few more steps, but they are still really straightforward.

Moderate: Have a few DIY projects under your belt already? These projects are perfect for you. There is nothing complicated or tricky, but a bit of experience might help.

Advanced: These projects have multiple steps and are a bit more complicated. You certainly don't have to be a master carpenter, but you should have a good working knowledge of tools and basic DIY techniques.

Wooden
Signs

Simple Framed Sign

Difficulty: Easy

Once you know the basic steps to making a simple framed wood sign, you can make gorgeous signs that say anything you want in absolutely any size, font, or color. And with this easy trick for transferring designs directly onto wood, you won't need perfect handwriting or an expensive cutting machine to make stencils, either. Soon, you'll be whipping up framed signs to decorate your own home, to give as gifts, and possibly even to sell. Trust me, it becomes pretty addicting! This is a great project to use up smaller scraps of plywood.

Materials

- ¾" plywood @ 11" x 11"
- 1" x 2" x 8' pine board
- 100-grit sandpaper
- White paint and brush
- Paper printout of text/design
- Tape
- Black oil-based paint marker, or black paint
- Stain
- Clean rags and/or brushes
- Finishing nails
- Wood glue
- Sawtooth picture hanger

Tools

- Pencil
- Saw
- Hammer or nail gun

Dimensions

This sign is a 12.5" square, including the frame. This exact process, modified accordingly, can be used to make a sign of any size.

Tip

You should always use ¾" plywood when making signs. It is tempting to use ¼" plywood when making signs because it is cheaper and you only need the front surface anyway, but this is a bad idea as the thinner plywood is much more difficult to properly attach to the frame, and it will also warp over time.

Steps

1. Once your plywood is cut to size in a square, sand away any rough edges.

2. Paint it white. You may need a couple of coats of paint.

3. Choose the words for your sign and a font you like. Adjust the sizing of your text to work with the size of the sign—in this case no larger than a single sheet of 8.5" x 11" copy paper—and print it out. Note: if you are making a sign with wording that is larger than a standard piece of printer paper, you can split the words up to print on several different sheets of paper or print it inexpensively at a local copy store as an engineer print.

4. It is very easy to transfer your printout design to the plywood using a simple pencil. Turn the printout over and use the pencil to shade lightly all over the back of the design. Then, place it faceup on the plywood, making sure to center the words where you want them on the wood. Gently tape the design in place, and then firmly trace around each letter with the pencil. When you remove the paper, a faint pencil outline of the design will remain on the wood.

5. Use a black paint marker to color or fill in the outlined letters. You can also use a small paintbrush and black paint, which requires more finesse.

6. To make the wooden frame, cut the 1" x 2" pine board into two 11" pieces and two 12.5" pieces. Note: If you are making a sign of a different size, cut two pieces that are the same length as the height of the sign and two pieces that are 1.5 inches longer than the width of the sign.

7. Sand any rough edges and then stain them with your stain of choice using a clean rag. This frame is stained using Minwax dark walnut.

8. Line up one of the shorter pieces with any side of your plywood sign and attach it with a couple of finishing nails using a hammer or nail gun. Attach the other short side to the opposite side of the sign.

9. Use finishing nails to attach the other two longer sides of the frame to the sign. It is a good idea to use wood glue in addition to a couple of nails in each corner to keep everything secure.

10. Add a sawtooth picture hanger to the back for hanging.

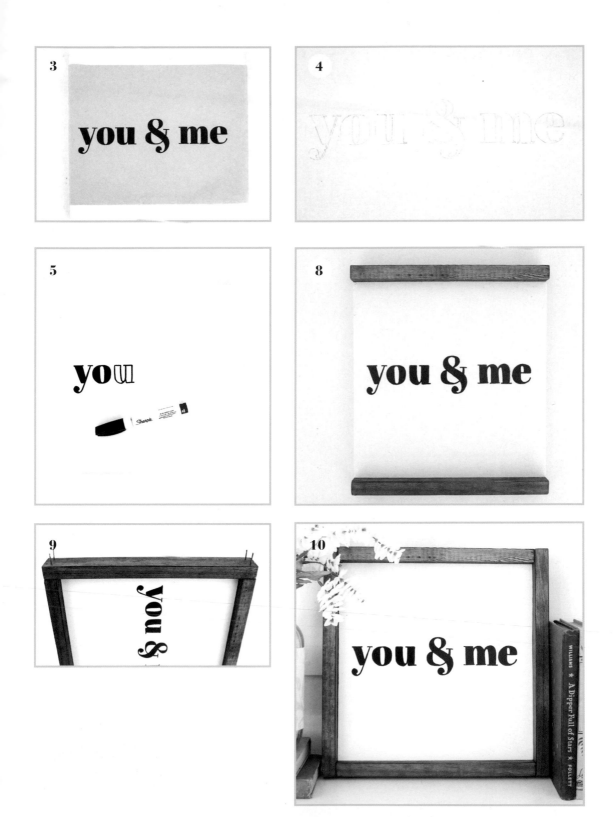

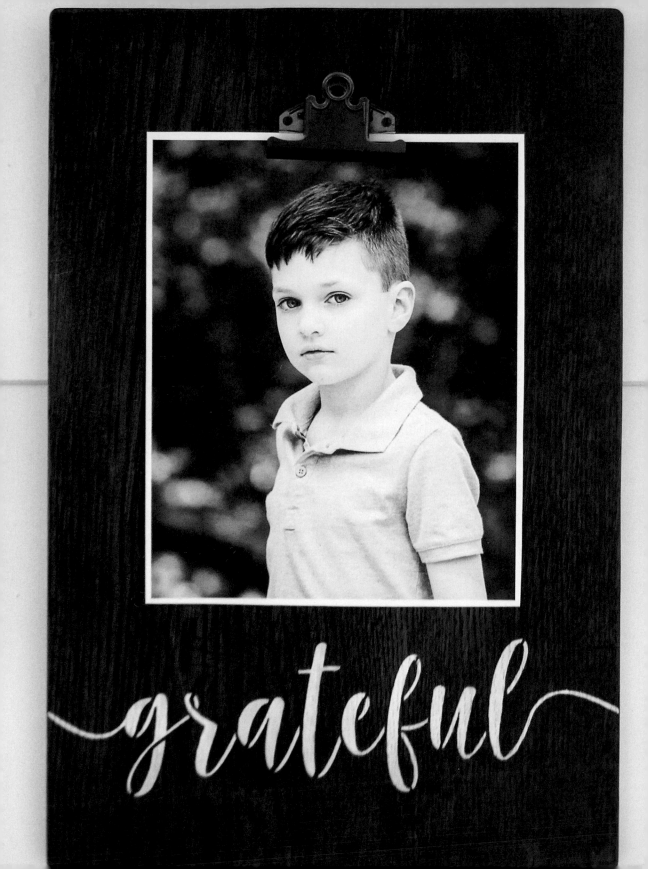

Stenciled Wooden Clipboard

Difficulty: Beginner

This stenciled clipboard makes a gorgeous display for your favorite photos or art prints. The attached clip makes it quick and easy for you to change out the photo, and the stenciled words can be customized to say whatever you want. If you can't find the right stencil, just use a simple pencil transfer technique, which will allow you to write whatever you want in any font you like. Not only will this look beautiful in your home; it also makes a fantastic personalized wedding or hostess gift.

Materials

- 11.5" x 19" wood plank (from a 1" x 12" board or ¾" plywood)
- 100-grit sandpaper
- Stain
- Clean rags and/or brushes
- Word stencil of your choice
- White paint
- Repositionable spray adhesive
- Cosmetics foam wedge sponge, or a stencil brush, or foam brush
- Small nails
- Clipboard clip
- Sawtooth picture hanger

Tools

- Saw
- Hammer

Dimensions

This sign is 11.5" wide and 19" tall, which works perfectly for holding an 8" x 10" photo or print.

Remember

All wood boards are actually smaller than their labeled size because they shrink in the drying process before they are sold. For example, a 2" x 4" is always 1.5" x 3.5".

Steps

1. Start by cutting your wood to size, 11.5" wide by 19" long. A small piece of a 1" x 12" board works perfectly for this, but you can also use a scrap of ¾" plywood or whatever other scrap wood you have on hand.

2. Sand the entire board so it is smooth and lightly round the corners of the board.

3. Stain the wood in the color of your choice using a clean rag. This sign is stained Minwax Dark Walnut.

4. You are ready to stencil on the word. (Note: if you can't find the right stencil, you can also use a simpler pencil transfer technique that will allow you to write whatever you want in any font you like—see page 14) There are a few tricks to getting perfectly crisp letters when stenciling. First, spray the stencil with repositionable adhesive. Carefully attach it to the wood plank, making sure it is positioned where you want it. Smooth the stencil down, making sure it is adhered to the wood well. This helps prevent paint from bleeding and smearing underneath the stencil.

5. The best tool for stenciling is a small foam wedge used for applying cosmetics (but you can also use a stencil brush or foam brush). Add a small amount of white paint to the flat side of the foam wedge and dab any excess off on a paper towel. Then, lightly dab the paint-stained foam wedge over the stencil. You do not want to use a lot of paint when stenciling; excess paint causes smears and smudges. Let the paint dry and then repeat the process to lay over a second coat of paint. Then, carefully peel off the stencil.

6. Attach your clipboard clip using a hammer and small nails. Remember to check that it is centered.

7. Attach a sawtooth picture hanger to the back and add your favorite photo.

3

4

5

6

7

Reclaimed Wood Sign

Difficulty: Moderate

Don't have space for an entire reclaimed wood wall? You can still add the beauty of reclaimed wood to your rooms with these signs. The reclaimed wood creates a beautiful background full of texture for any message you choose. You can cut out the word yourself with a scroll saw, but you can also find them pre-cut at craft supply stores. If you don't have a picture frame, you can also make your own using 1" x 2" boards.

Materials

- Reclaimed wood planks of varying finishes
- Picture frame
- 100-grit sandpaper
- White paint and brush (optional)
- Stain and clean rag or brush (optional)
- 2 thin strips of ¼" wood (lattice works well for this)
- Wood glue
- 1" wood screws or tacks
- 1" x 1" square wood dowels to extend the back of the frame (optional)
- Finishing nails
- "Thankful" word cutout
- 2 d-ring picture hangers and picture hanging wire

Tools

- Safety glasses
- Hearing protection
- Tape measure
- Pencil
- Saw
- Drill and drill bits
- Hammer or nail gun
- Screwdriver

Dimensions

This sign can be made in absolutely any size. Here, my sign is in an 18" x 24" frame.

Steps

1. Gather your reclaimed and scrap wood and arrange the pieces in different combinations until you find the ones you like. If you don't have wood in different finishes, use paint and stain to add some variety.

2. Here, I use an old picture frame, but you can also build your own basic wood frame pretty easily from 1" x 2" wood following steps 6–9 in the "Simple Framed Sign" project (page 13).

3. Turn your frame over and measure the dimensions of its opening. Arrange your reclaimed and scrap wood in the order you want and cut the pieces to the frame opening's height and width with a saw. Sand any rough edges.

4. If you'd like, paint your picture frame white.

5. Make sure the wood pieces fit well into the frame. You may need to do a bit of trimming or extra sanding to get a good fit. Turn the wood pieces facedown on your work surface.

6. From your remaining reclaimed wood, cut two additional thin strips of wood that are slightly shorter by about 2" than the width of the frame opening. For my 18" x 24" frame, I cut wood strips that were 22" long. Lay the two strips horizontally along the back of the vertical wood pieces, one near the top and one near the bottom. Predrill holes into each strip, one hole aligned to each vertical piece. Use wood glue to keep the pieces in place, then use 1" wood screws or tacks to attach each plank to the two strips.

7. Place the wood plank sign in the back of your frame. If you are repurposing a picture frame, the wood plank sign's width may extend past the back of the frame since wood planks are much thicker than photos or art prints. This won't be visible from the front but may be visible from the side depending on where you hang your sign.

8. If this is the case, you may want to add some trim to hide the rough edges of your wood planks. Use 1" x 1" wood to make a small frame to hide the edges of the wood from sight. Cut two pieces of 1" x 1" wood the same length as the two longer sides of your wood plank sign. and two pieces of 1" x 1" wood 2" longer than the shorter sides of the sign. Paint the 1" x 1" wood to match your frame and attach them to the back of the frame using a hammer and finishing nails.

9. Paint your word cutout if needed. Turn the frame over. Use wood glue to glue the word cutout in place on the wood background.

10. Use a screwdriver to attach two d-rings to the back. These should be attached on either side of the frame approximately one-third of the way down from the top.

Angle the d-rings slightly toward the center of the frame.

11. Cut a piece of picture wire twice the width of the frame. Loop the picture wire through each d-ring and twist the two ends firmly together in the middle. Make sure the wire is not so long it shows above the frame when hanging.

Wood Plank Photo Board

Difficulty: Easy

This beautiful, rustic photo board provides an easy way to showcase a rotating gallery of family photos or favorite art prints. Just clip them on and off for a quick and easy change. Make a single frame to hold a special photo, or create a gallery of three to make a big impact on a blank wall.

Materials

- Four 1" x 2" x 8' furring strips
- 100-grit sandpaper
- White paint and chip brush
- Stain
- Mineral spirits
- Clean rags and/or brushes
- Plastic putty knife
- Wood glue
- Two 17" strips of ¼"-thick wood (lattice works well)
- ½" wood screws or tacks
- Twine
- 2 mini clothespins
- Sawtooth picture hanger

Tools

- Safety glasses
- Hearing protection
- Tape measure
- Pencil
- Miter saw or other saw
- Staple gun (optional) or duct tape

Dimensions

The final photo display is an 18" square, a size that works well for 11" x 14" photos. The measurements of this project can be easily adapted to hold different-sized photos and prints.

Steps

1. Cut the 1" x 2" wood planks into twelve 18" strips. Sand any rough edges.

2. You can finish your planks any way you choose. The finish on these planks was created using two different methods, both of which use white paint and a mix of Minwax Jacobean stain and Minwax Classic Gray stain.

   a. The first method involves dry-brushing a small amount of white paint over the wood using a chip brush or another brush to create a weathered, layered finish. Put a very small amount of paint on your brush and then wipe as much of it off against the lip of the paint can as possible—you want your brush to be as dry as possible with just a bit of paint. To remove even more paint, you can wipe your brush on a paper towel several times. Then, lightly brush the paint across the wood.

   b. Once the paint has dried, use a clean rag to wipe wood stain all over the wood, including the painted parts. Immediately afterward, use a second clean rag dipped in mineral spirits to wipe away the excess stain. After every few wipes, begin with a fresh section of the rag. This will remove the stain from the painted areas while allowing it to penetrate any raw wood that is exposed.

   c. The second method is similar but gives a more heavily painted finish. Load a small dab of paint onto a plastic putty knife and drag it over the wood to apply the paint randomly.

   d. Let the paint dry fully and then use the same stain and mineral spirits application described in step 2b. This gives an authentic chippy paint effect.

3. Once your planks have fully dried, lay them out in a square, finding an arrangement of the various finishes that you like. Then, turn the planks upside down. Apply wood glue between each plank to help secure them together.

4. Lay the two thin 17" wood strips across the back of the square. These will connect the wood strips. Use wood glue to attach the two strips firmly to each plank.

1

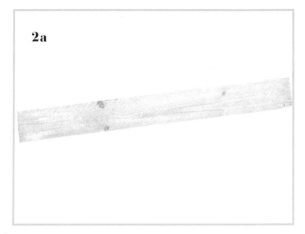

2a

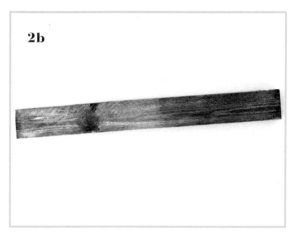

2b

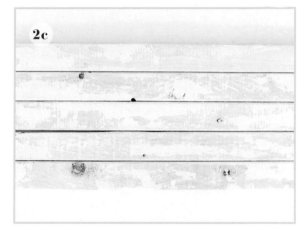

2c

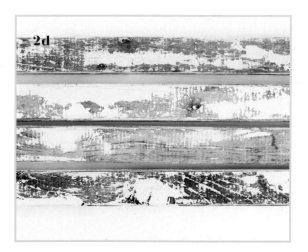

2d

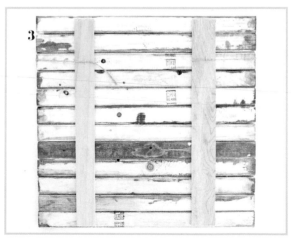

3

5. Use ½" wood screws or tacks to further secure everything together, especially if you think your photo displays may end up getting knocked around. However, wood glue should also be enough to hold everything in place nicely.

6. Cut a piece of twine around 2 feet long. Stretch the twine across the front of your sign and then wrap the two ends around to the back. You can staple these ends to the back with a staple gun or simply tape them with duct tape.

7. Clip 2 mini clothespins to the twine running along the front.

8. Attach a sawtooth picture hanger to the back. Add a favorite photo and hang.

6

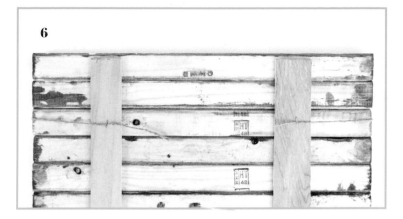

7

8

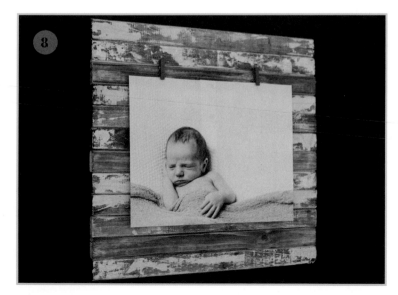

Rustic Pallet Wood Sign

Difficulty: Easy

Looking for a slightly more rustic vintage-style sign? This pallet sign, which is extremely easy to make, is a fun way to add texture and warmth to any blank wall. If you don't have pallet wood, use any rustic boards you can find. Here, you'll learn another great method for transferring text to wood.

Materials

- Three 1" x 6" x 30" wood planks (pallet wood or any rustic wood)
- 100-grit sandpaper
- Two 13" wood planks (any scrap wood will work because this won't be seen)
- 1¼" screws
- Stain and clean rags and/or brush (optional)
- Printout of your text in any font
- Chalk
- Tape
- White paint and small paintbrush, or oil-based paint pen
- Sawtooth picture hanger

Tools

- Safety glasses
- Hearing protection
- Tape measure
- Pencil
- Saw
- Drill and drill bits

Dimensions

The final sign is 30" wide and 16.5" high. Feel free to adapt the method below to make signs of any size.

Steps

1. Sand the three 1" x 6" x 30" pieces of wood to remove any rough edges.

2. Lay the three 1" x 6" wood planks facedown on a flat surface. Place the two smaller 13" pieces of wood along the back and use wood screws to attach them to each of the wood planks. Be sure to predrill your holes to prevent the wood from splitting.

3. Stain your wood if you'd like.

4. Once your new finish is completely dry, it is time to add the text. You can always hand letter your wording or use a stencil directly onto the wood, but you can also easily transfer any design that is printed off from the computer. Print out your desired text and design. Adjust the size up or down as needed until it is the perfect size for your wood.

5. Rub chalk all over the back of your printed design. Then, tape your design, front-side up, to the wood sign, making sure to position your words carefully.

6. Use a pencil to trace around each letter. Remove the paper—you'll see that a chalk outline of your design has transferred onto the wood.

7. Carefully use a small artist's paintbrush to outline and fill in each letter with white paint. You can also use an oil-based paint pen for easier lettering on a painted or recently stained background. Unfortunately, paint pens often don't work as well on reclaimed, weathered wood.

8. Secure a sawtooth picture hanger to the back of the sign. You're ready to hang it up.

1

2

5 Stay Awhile

6

7 Stay Awhile

8 Stay Awhile

United States Outline Sign

Difficulty: Moderate

Are you looking for a fun way to mark out your latest road trip? Or are you just feeling patriotic? This rustic sign featuring the outline of the United States is the perfect decoration for your walls. You can keep it simple as a statement art piece or personalize it with decorative tacks marking the places that are special to you. You can also paint on messages to give it a more patriotic spin, such as "From Sea to Shining Sea" or "Land That I Love." However you choose to display it, this piece will add warmth and texture to any space.

Materials

- Pallet wood or two 1" x 4" x 8' furring strips
- ¼" plywood @ 2' x 4'
- Wood glue
- Outline of the United States to use as a pattern
- 100-grit sandpaper
- Paint and brush (optional)
- Stain and clean rag (optional)
- Sawtooth picture hanger

Tools

- Safety glasses
- Hearing protection
- Tape measure
- Pencil
- Circular saw or table saw (optional)
- Projector (optional)
- Marker
- Jigsaw

Dimensions

The final sign is 19" by 30". You can adjust these measurements to make a larger or smaller sign.

Steps

1. Cut the pallet wood into nine planks that are 22" long. If you are using furring strips, cut eight planks that are 22" long and use one of the scrap pieces as a shorter ninth plank. When you arrange the planks, place this shorter plank on the top-right to cover the small northeast section of the US outline.

2. Cut the plywood to approximately 22" x 30". If you do not have a circular saw or table saw, you can get it cut in the store when you buy your plywood.

3. Use wood glue to attach the wood planks to the top of the plywood. Allow the glue to completely dry.

4. Trace an outline of the United States onto the wood planks using a marker. One method is to use a projector to project the outline onto the wood and simply trace it. The second method is to print a map on a poster at a copy store at the appropriate size (you can do this very inexpensively). Cut out the outline and trace it onto the wood.

5. Use a jigsaw to cut out the outline. Remember to work in small sections and cut carefully. It is easiest to cut out the general shape first, and then cut the finer details.

6. Sand any rough edges after cutting. If there are traces of marker still visible on the wood after cutting, sand these off.

7. You may finish your sign with any paint or stain color you choose. This version is finished using Minwax Provincial stain applied with a clean rag. Remember that stains may look different on different types of wood.

8. Attach a sawtooth picture hanger to the back. You're ready to hang it up.

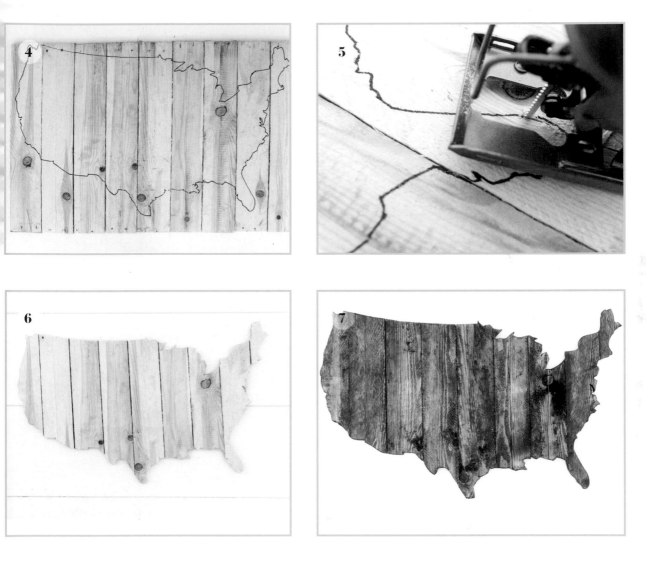

Wall Décor

Rustic Barnwood Frame

Difficulty: Easy

Unique picture frames with lots of character are usually very expensive and hard to find. Luckily, here is how to make your own! This barnwood frame is quick and easy to make in just about any size, and you can also use it to decorate a home in many different ways—frame a favorite art print, attach a chalkboard to the back for writing, or use an oversized version to frame a plain bathroom mirror.

Materials

- 8' barnwood or 1" x 4" x 8' furring strip
- 100-grit sandpaper
- Wood glue
- Four 2.5" metal corner braces
- Black acrylic craft paint, or black chalkboard paint, and a small paintbrush
- Sixteen ½" wood screws
- Sawtooth picture hanger
- ¼" plywood, cut to the dimensions of the frame (optional)
- Picture mat and poster board, according to the dimensions of the frame (optional)

Tools

- Safety glasses
- Hearing protection
- Tape measure
- Pencil
- Miter saw
- Drill and drill bits

Dimensions

The final square frame is approximately 20" by 20".

Tip

This is the perfect project for reclaimed wood with great texture—but you can also work with new wood.

Steps

1. Choose an interesting piece of wood that is fairly even and not warped or bent. If using reclaimed wood, be sure to clean it well before using. If using newer wood, furring strips are a great choice because they typically have lots of texture, knotholes, and other imperfections. Adding any kind of stain will further emphasize the interesting imperfections of the wood. The wood used here is 4.5" wide, but other sizes will also work.

2. Use a miter saw to cut a 45-degree angle at one end of your wood. Measure 20" on the long side and cut another 45-degree angle at the other end to make a trapezoid (see picture). Repeat to make four sides of the frame.

3. Sand any rough edges.

4. Arrange the pieces into a frame to make sure all the joints match up. When working with reclaimed wood, it can sometimes be a bit difficult to match up the mitered edges, and you may need to make additional small cuts or sand certain areas to get a good fit.

5. Use wood glue to attach the wood pieces together.

6. The corner braces typically have a shiny steel appearance, so to make them more rustic, paint them with a matte black paint. Acrylic craft paint or chalkboard paint work well.

7. Position the first corner brace on top of one corner of the frame, centered in the middle of where the edges meet. Drill holes into the wood for the screws. Screw in the wood screws.

8. Paint the screws black to match the braces.

9. Attach a sawtooth picture hanger to the back of the frame.

10. At this stage, you may choose to hang the empty frame as it is to add texture to a gallery wall. You could also paint a piece of ¼" plywood (cut to the dimensions of the back of the frame) with the black chalkboard paint and nail it to the back of the frame to make a framed chalkboard. Alternatively, you can frame an art print. Layer your art with a picture mat if desired and center it in the frame. Staple a piece of poster board or cardboard to the back of the frame behind the art to keep it in place.

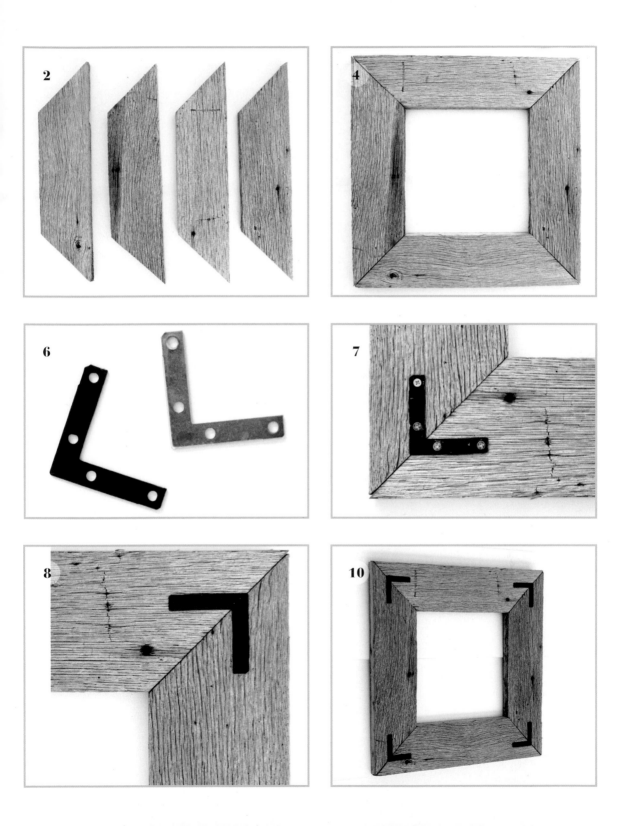

Scrap Wood Sunburst Mirror

Difficulty: Moderate

When your pile of scrap wood starts getting out of control, this mirror is the perfect project for turning it into something beautiful. You can use scraps of plywood, pieces of wood planks, or a variety of reclaimed wood. This version has a coastal weathered finish, but it would also look lovely painted all white or stained in various shades.

Materials

- Scrap wood, no more than 1" thick
- Various paints and chip brush
- Stain and clean rag
- 100-grit sandpaper
- 8" round mirror
- ¼" plywood for backing, at least 12" x 12"
- Wood glue
- Sawtooth picture hanger
- Strong adhesive (make sure it is mirror safe)
- 1.5 yards thin braided rope or twine

Tools

- Safety glasses
- Hearing protection
- Tape measure
- Pencil
- Jigsaw
- Hammer

Dimensions

The final mirror is approximately 26" in diameter.

Steps

1. You can choose to paint or stain your wood scraps either before or after cutting them to shape. To achieve the finish shown, I applied golden oak stain, white paint, light gray paint, dark gray paint, and turquoise paint before the wood was cut. Dry-brushing different combinations of the colors onto each piece of wood using a chip brush gives a variety of finishes.

2. Cut your wood scraps into various types of triangles (and quadrangles) that are 9 to 10" long. These four basic shapes work well.

3. Use sandpaper to smooth any rough edges.

4. Use a jigsaw to cut the ¼" plywood backing into a circle approximately 12" in diameter.

5. Once you have several pieces cut, start laying them out around the mirror, against the plywood. Try to avoid using the exact same shape or paint finish next to each other. Keep moving things around until you are happy with the layout. As you continue to fill in the pieces, you may need to be more purposeful about cutting specific shapes and sizes to fill the gaps.

6. Use wood glue to attach the wood pieces, which you've already laid out in the desired formation, to the plywood backing. It is also a good idea to add some wood glue between the wood pieces.

7. Attach a sawtooth picture hanger to the back on the plywood. We do this before adding the mirror to prevent accidentally shattering the mirror when attaching the hanger.

8. Use a mirror-safe adhesive to attach the mirror to the front of the frame.

9. Glue the thin rope around the edge of the mirror two times, tucking in the final end.

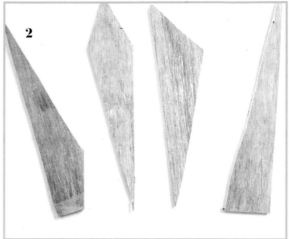

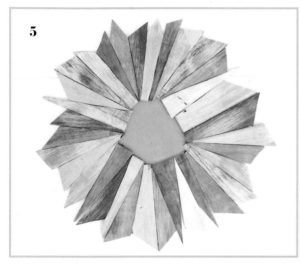

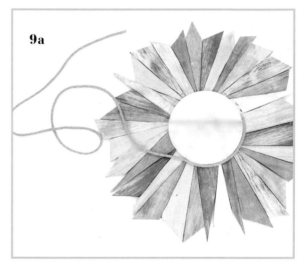

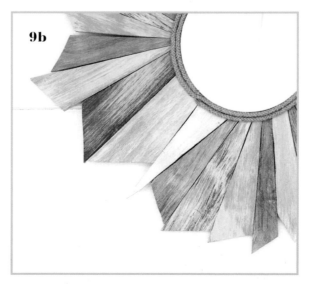

Weathered Wall Vase Hangers

Difficulty: Beginner

Flowers make everything beautiful—so why not hang them on the wall? These gorgeous wall vases are quick and easy to make, and they add fantastic character and texture to any wall. You can make several to hang in a group, or just make one and add it to a fun farmhouse-style gallery wall.

Materials

- Reclaimed wood or a rustic wood plank, at least 6" wide
- Glass bottles
- Wood glue
- Finishing nails
- 100-grit sandpaper
- Copper pipe straps that fit the neck of the bottle
- Copper tacks
- Sawtooth picture hangers
- Flowers or small branches

Tools

- Safety glasses
- Hearing protection
- Tape measure
- Pencil
- Saw
- Hammer

Dimensions

Each piece of wood is 7" x 12". The bottles shown are 5" tall.

Steps

1. Cut your wood plank to the dimensions you want your wall vase hangers to be. It has to be tall enough to accommodate the height of the bottle as well as the flowers sticking out, and wide enough for the width of the bottle with space between. If you are making several wall hangers, cut all of the wood at the same time.

2. Lay one of your bottles flat (horizontally) on a piece of cut wood. Measure the distance from the surface of the wood to the neck of the bottle. Cut a small scrap of wood for each wall vase hanger with this measurement for one side, and 2" on the other side. It is best to use the same type of wood so it blends into the background.

3. Use wood glue and a couple of small nails to attach the small wood piece to the wood base, where the neck of the bottle will rest.

4. Use sandpaper to smooth any rough edges.

5. You are going to use the copper tacks to attach the copper pipe fitting to the small piece of wood. It is very difficult to nail the copper tacks directly into the wood, so first nail a couple of finishing nails into the wood where the holes need to be. Then, remove these nails. Position the copper strap around your bottle neck and nail the copper tacks into the previously nailed holes.

6. Add a picture hanger to the back for hanging. Hang it up.

7. Finally, place the flowers or small branches you like—faux or real—in the bottles.

Reclaimed Wood Wreath

Difficulty: Moderate

This nontraditional wreath will make a huge statement wherever you hang it. Suitable for any season, it'll look beautiful hanging on a front door, a blank wall, or as part of a rustic gallery wall. The flower can easily be swapped out for different types of greenery or even a rustic bow for the different seasons of the year.

Materials

- Reclaimed wood scraps in various widths, textures, and finishes
- Paint and chip brush (optional)
- Stain and clean rag (optional)
- 100-grit sandpaper
- ¼" plywood (at least 20" x 20")
- Wood glue
- 5/8" wood screws
- Sawtooth picture hanger
- Faux flower and leaves (optional)
- Fishing line (optional)

Tools

- Safety glasses
- Hearing protection
- Tape measure
- Pencil
- Jigsaw
- Drill and drill bits

Dimensions

The finished wreath is approximately 18" in diameter.

Steps

1. Gather your reclaimed wood with a variety of textures, finishes, and widths, and try out a few different arrangements. If you aren't happy with how it looks, you can always use paint or stain to add more character to your wood.

2. Draw a large circle onto the wood to make the outline of the wreath. The easiest way to do this is to trace the circle using a large bucket, charger, or anything else that is round. This wreath is 18" wide, but your wreath can be any dimension you prefer. Use a jigsaw to cut each board along the circle line.

3. Draw a smaller circle for the outline of the hole in the center of the wreath. This wreath has a 9.5" hole. Cut it out with the jigsaw.

4. Smooth any rough edges with sandpaper.

5. On the ¼" plywood, which is going to be the wreath backing, draw a circle that is around 1" smaller than the circumference of your wreath. This is so that the plywood won't be seen from the front or the side once it is attached to the back. Cut out the circle with a jigsaw.

6. Draw a small circle on the plywood that is around 1" larger than the inner circle of your wreath. Again, this is so that the plywood won't be seen from the front or the side. To cut the inner circle, drill a pilot hole into the small circle that you will be discarding using a drill and your largest drill bit. Slip the jigsaw blade into the hole and then cut as usual.

7. Lay out the boards for your wreath facedown on a flat surface. Make sure all of the edges line up well. Attach the plywood backing with wood glue and ¾" screws.

8. Add a sawtooth picture hanger to the back and hang.

9. You can leave your wreath like this if you prefer. To soften the wreath, you can easily add a burlap bow or a faux flower. Attach your bow or flowers permanently with hot glue. For a more temporary decoration, tie them on using a fishing line, which is nearly invisible and holds everything on securely. This way, you can easily switch out the décor on your wreath as the seasons change.

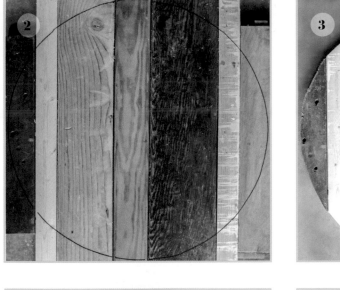

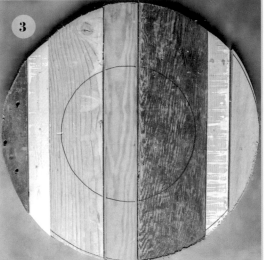

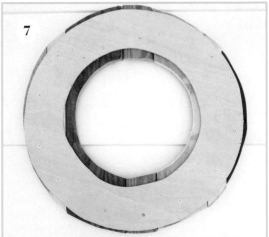

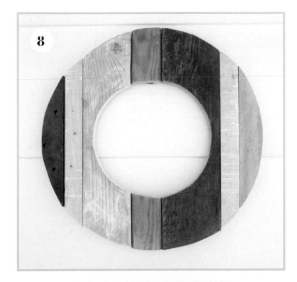

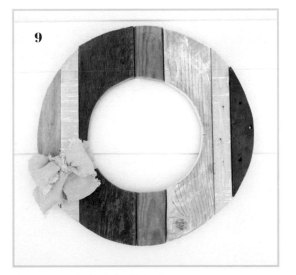

Rustic Barnwood Quilt

Difficulty: Advanced

If you drive along country roads in some parts of the United States, you may see big painted wooden quilt squares hanging on old barns. This smaller barnwood quilt is inspired by those old wood quilts. This quilt square gets its beauty from using a mix of reclaimed wood of different finishes and textures.

Materials

- Various scrap pieces of reclaimed wood planks (1" x 4" works great)
- ¼" plywood @ 2' x 2'
- 100-grit sandpaper
- Wood glue
- 1" x 2" x 8' furring strip
- Paint and brush (optional)
- Stain and clean rag (optional)
- Finishing nails
- Sawtooth picture hanger

Tools

- Safety glasses
- Hearing protection
- Tape measure
- Pencil
- Miter saw
- Jigsaw
- Hammer or nail gun

Dimensions

The final piece is a square of 25.5" x 25.5".

Tip

Remember, 1" x 4" wood planks are actually 0.75" x 3.5".

Steps

1. Begin by gathering your reclaimed wood planks of any size—1" x 4" wood planks work great. Choose a variety of different wood tones and finishes. If you don't have many varied finishes or wood types to begin with, create your own variety by staining and painting different pieces in different ways. You can choose to include painted wood pieces or stick with only stained and natural wood. You can use wood that is of the same thickness for a uniform surface or use woods of varying thicknesses to give the final piece depth and texture.

2. The 2' x 2' plywood will form the base of the barn quilt. Measure and draw a vertical straight line down the center of the wood. Repeat in the other direction to draw another horizontal line so that the plywood is divided into four equal sections.

3. Now, it's time to cut all the wood pieces. Cutting may look like it will take a lot of time, but it goes by more quickly than it looks. Before you start, if any of your wood planks are more than 3.5" wide, cut them down to 3.5" first (the size of a 1" x 4" board).

4. Then, set your miter saw to 45 degrees and make a cut at one end across the width. After the first cut, move your plank down 3" and make another parallel cut. (There is likely a ruler built into your miter saw which makes these 3" cuts go very quickly.) Continue to do this until you reach the end of the board or have enough pieces of that type of wood. You will need 40 pieces cut to this size. These will later form the X in the center of the wood quilt.

5. Next, cut the pieces for the sides that will surround the X. To do this, cut your scraps of wood to 2" wide. Then, make the same 45-degree angle cut at one end. You will need 24 pieces of this shape in different lengths: 8 pieces that are 8" long, 8 pieces that are 6" long, and 8 pieces that are 4" long. Sand off any rough edges.

6. On the plywood, lay out your 40 quadrilateral pieces that you cut in step 4 to form an X, making sure to vary the finishes as you arrange them. The first 8 pieces should line up with the vertical and horizontal lines you drew on the plywood earlier in the shape of a +. Then, continue laying the rest of the pieces as shown in the shape of an X.

7. Once you have a layout you are happy with, glue the wood pieces to the plywood one at a time. When you get near the edges of the board, you will need to use a pencil to mark the excess that needs to be cut off, and then carefully cut it with a jigsaw.

4

6a

6b

8. Arrange the 24 long pieces you cut in step 5 around the X until you are happy with the arrangement.

9. Before gluing each piece, mark where it needs to be cut in order to line up with the edges of the plywood, and cut it with a jigsaw.

10. Finally, you will need to cut a few very small triangles and squares to complete the gaps in the square. It is tempting to try to cut these from very small scraps of wood, but that is extremely difficult to do. It is better to cut these from larger pieces of wood using the miter saw or jigsaw. Remember to sand off any splinters and rough edges before attaching them.

11. Once all of the pieces are glued to the plywood, it is time to create the frame.

Cut the 1" x 2" furring strips into two pieces that are 24" long each and two pieces that are 25.5" long each. Sand the rough edges.

12. Finish these with the stain or paint of your choice. This frame is finished with Minwax special walnut stain.

13. Line one of the shorter pieces up with one side of your quilt and attach it with a couple of finishing nails. Attach the other shorter piece to the opposite side of the quilt.

14. Use finishing nails to attach the other two sides of the frame to the quilt. It is a good idea to use wood glue along with a couple of nails in each corner to keep everything secure.

15. Add a sawtooth picture hanger to the back and hang.

Oversized Farmhouse Clock

Difficulty: Advanced

Huge farmhouse-style clocks have become very popular. As everything becomes more digital in our world, I believe we are really starting to embrace the beauty of physical things like a simple wooden clockface. This oversized clock really makes a statement wherever you hang it. It will look impressive hanging over a mantel or on a focal wall, and it also serves a practical function, allowing you to see the time from anywhere in the room.

Materials

- Three 1" x 4" x 8' furring strips
- Nail and piece of twine or string (optional)
- 100-grit sandpaper
- ¼" plywood @ 2' x 4'
- Clock kit with 12" hands
- White paint
- Stain
- Mineral spirits
- Clean rags and/or brushes
- Wood glue
- ¾" wood screws
- Printout of Roman numerals
- Medium-tip black oil-based paint pen
- 2 d-ring picture hangers and picture hanging wire

Tools

- Safety glasses
- Hearing protection
- Tape measure
- Pencil
- Circular saw
- Router or chisel and hammer
- Jigsaw
- Drill and drill bits

Dimensions

The finished clock is 32" in diameter.

Steps

1. Cut the 1" x 4" planks into nine pieces, 32" long each. Arrange them next to one another to form a square. If any of your wood pieces are a little short, just put them on the ends.

2. Trace a large circle, 32" across, onto the boards using a pencil. If you don't have anything large enough to trace, make a circle shape yourself: Hammer a nail into the center of the middle board. Tie one end of a piece of twine or string to the nail, and tie the other end to a pencil, leaving exactly 16" of twine between the nail and pencil. Keeping the string taut, draw a circle with the pencil onto the boards.

3. Use a jigsaw to cut out the circle. Sand the edges to remove any splinters and rough edges. Number each plank on the back with a pencil. This will make it much easier to know where each piece goes when it is time to reassemble the circle.

4. From the plywood, cut a circle that is just slightly smaller than the clockface—It will serve as a backing to keep everything firmly attached. To draw your circle on the plywood, you can trace the wood plank circle onto the plywood, then draw a circle within it that is about 1" smaller all around. Cut this shape out with the jigsaw and sand any rough edges with sandpaper.

5. Most clock kits are made to fit very thin clockfaces, not thick pieces of wood. You will need to cut out a space in the wood for the clock mechanism to fit. Take the center plank from your clockface and measure out the exact center of the board. This should also be the center of the whole clockface. Drill a hole through the board in the center that is large enough for the shaft that holds the clock hands to stick through.

6. Next, mark a 4" square in the center of the same board, making sure that your clock mechanism is not any larger than the square. The edges of the wood plank will form two sides of the square and you will cut the other two sides. You aren't going to cut all of the way through the wood; you are simply cutting away a square from the back to make the wood here thinner. If you do not have a router, use a circular saw, a chisel, and a hammer. Set the blade depth of your circular saw to ½". Turn your board facedown and use your circular saw to cut the two sides of the square you previously marked. Make several more parallel cuts between the initial two cuts. The use a chisel and hammer to remove the wood between the jigsaw cuts.

7. You will also need to cut a matching hole in the plywood. Draw a 4" square in the center of the plywood backing you already cut out. Use your largest drill bit to drill a pilot hole and then insert your jigsaw blade and cut out the square.

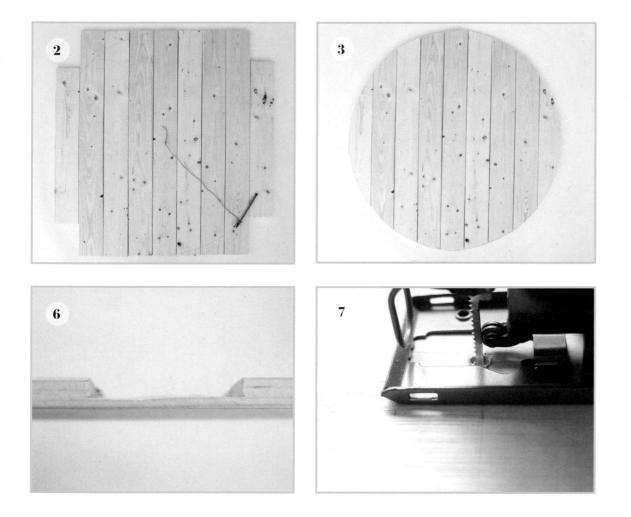

8. You can paint your clock however you want. For a simple weathered, white finish, paint each of the planks with two coats of white paint. Be sure to also paint the edges.

9. Once the paint has dried completely, sand each plank to rough up the paint finish. Make sure to especially focus your sanding around the edges of each plank and near any knots and imperfections in the wood.

10. Use a clean rag to wipe stain onto the painted planks. Then immediately use a second clean rag to wipe the entire thing down with mineral spirits. Use a clean section of the rag each time you wipe it. You may need to make a second pass with the mineral spirits to remove all of the excess stain from the paint. The dark stain will stick to all of the areas where raw wood is exposed but not the white paint, and you will be left with a beautifully aged white finish.

11. Arrange the planks back into a circle shape facedown. Follow the numbers you wrote on the backs as a guide.

12. Place the plywood backing on top, making sure to align the two holes you cut. Attach the backing to the clock using wood glue and screws.

13. To make the clock numbers, use a Roman numeral stencil if you have one. Simply tape the stencil in place for each numeral and use a black paint pen to trace the numeral outlines onto the clockface. If you use this method, skip steps 14–17. If you don't have a stencil, print out Roman numerals in your preferred font and size. This will be your template that will help you transfer the numerals onto the wood. For this clock, numerals that are around 4" high work well.

14. Cut a rectangular shape, leaving a small margin, around each number. To transfer the numerals to the wood, lightly color the back of each numeral with a pencil, making sure to color slightly beyond each numeral's outline.

15. Position the numerals around your clockface. When placing your numbers, it is easiest to place the 12, 3, 6, and 9 first. Make sure they are straight and approximately the same distance from the edge of the clock. Then, using those numbers as your guides, add the rest of the numbers.

16. Tape the numeral in place and firmly trace the outline of the numeral through the top of the printout and against the wood.

17. The pencil outline will be transferred onto the surface of your clock.

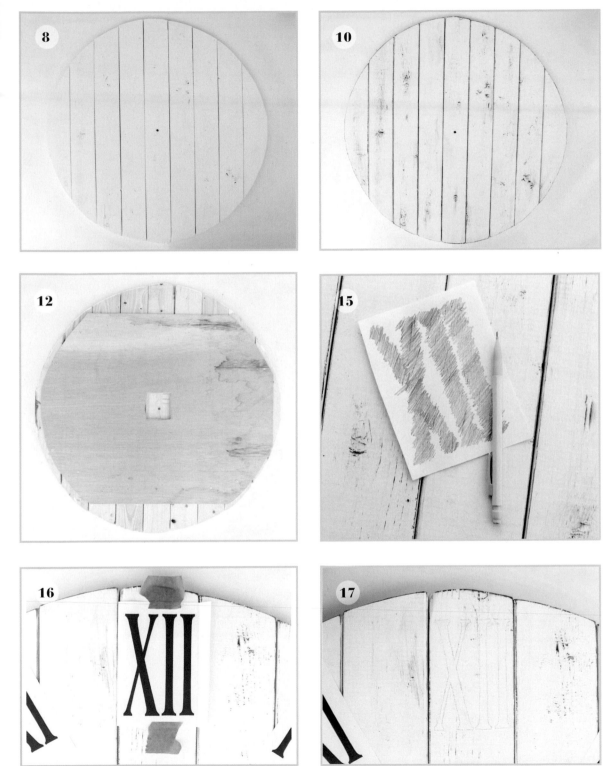

18. Use a medium-tip black oil-based paint marker to fill in each Roman numeral.

19. Add your clock mechanism and clock hands according to the instructions provided by the manufacturer.

20. Finally, screw the 2 d-rings to the back of the clock. These should be attached on either side of the clock approximately one-third of the way down from the top. Angle the d-rings slightly toward the center of the frame. Cut a piece of picture wire twice the width of the clock. Loop the picture wire through each d-ring and twist the two ends firmly together in the middle. Make sure the wire is not so long that it shows above the clock when hanging.

Home Décor

Herb Garden Planter Box

Difficulty: Beginner

This gorgeous planter box is super easy, taking less than thirty minutes to make! The best part is the whole box is made from one board of wood, requiring only a couple of simple cuts. Use it to plant a kitchen herb garden or simply fill it with mason jars full of flowers for a beautiful table centerpiece.

Materials

- 1" x 6" x 8' pine board
- 100-grit sandpaper
- White paint
- Stain
- Mineral spirits
- Matte sealer
- Clean rags and/or brushes
- Wood glue
- Finishing nails
- Plastic liner

Tools

- Safety glasses
- Hearing protection
- Tape measure
- Pencil
- Saw
- Hammer or nail gun
- Staple gun

Dimensions

The finished box is 2' long and 7" wide.

Tip

Look for a board that is straight but with plenty of rough spots and knotholes.

Steps

1. Start by cutting your 1" x 6" board into two 24" pieces, one 22.5" piece, and two 5.5" pieces.

2. To give your planter box a farmhouse look, sand all of the edges and corners to soften the newness.

3. To get a weathered white paint effect, start by painting a quick coat of white paint on your boards. Don't worry about covering the wood grain or getting into the little knotholes and rough spots. Let the paint dry and then lightly sand the wood with sandpaper to expose some of the raw wood and wood grain.

4. Use a clean rag to wipe on a coat of stain. Immediately, go back over the wood with a second clean rag dipped in mineral spirits. This will take most of the stain off the white paint, while leaving the stain on any bits of bare wood that are peeking through. Use a clean section of the rag each time you wipe it. You'll never guess this was a brand-new board twenty minutes ago.

5. Be sure to use a good sealer on top of your paint finish. A matte or flat sealer works best for a weathered finish.

6. Start to build the box. Attach one of the 24" boards to the two 5.5" side boards using wood glue and a nail in each corner. Make sure to attach the two shorter boards behind the long board rather than beside it.

7. Slide the 22.5" bottom board into place. It should fit snugly. If it is a bit too big, you can sand it down a little.

8. With the bottom in place, use wood glue and nails to attach the final 24" side. The pressure of the sides should keep the bottom in place perfectly, but if it feels a little loose, add a couple of nails along the bottom to reinforce it.

9. If you want to use this as a pretty centerpiece lined with mason jars, you are finished.

10. If you want to create an indoor herb garden, there are just a few more steps. Since this will be indoors, it won't have the typical drainage holes most planters have. Instead, staple a plastic lining inside the wooden box to help contain the water. To create drainage, add a thick layer of rocks to the bottom of the planter before adding soil. This gives the water room to drain away from the plant roots.

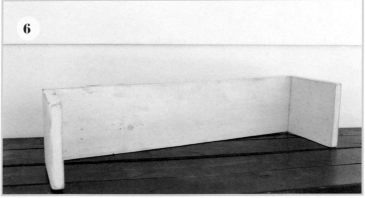

Vintage Doorknob Wall Hooks

Difficulty: Beginner

These wall hooks, which use vintage doorknobs, truly celebrate the beauty of reclaimed materials. Of course, you can take this simple idea and make it a dozen different ways using different types of knobs and hardware. These work amazingly well for hanging almost anything—jackets and bookbags in an entryway, towels in a bathroom, or scarves and jewelry in a bedroom.

Materials

- Pretty wood plank of any type
- Vintage doorknobs
- Hex bolts that fit the doorknobs
- Sawtooth picture hanger

Tools

- Safety glasses
- Hearing protection
- Tape measure
- Pencil
- Saw (if the wood needs to be cut)
- Drill and drill bits

Dimensions

For this project, you can use wood of any size your heart desires. For reference, the wood shown is 20" x 5.5".

Tip

This is a great project for any scraps of wood you may have that are particularly pretty or interesting. If you don't have great-looking wood, just use stain or paint to make a boring piece more attractive.

Steps

1. Cut the wood to your preferred length. The wood shown here is 20" and perfect for a small set of three doorknobs. If you'd like to make a larger piece with more doorknobs, lay your knobs along the wood to determine what size works best. You can use any number of knobs you want, but in general odd numbers look more appealing.

2. Remove extra pieces from your doorknobs until you are left with just the knob itself. Take all your doorknobs (because vintage hardware comes in different sizes) to a hardware store and find hex bolts that are the correct size to screw into them. Choose bolts that are slightly longer than the thickness of your wood. For example, if you are using wood that is ¾" thick, 1" hex bolts should work well.

3. Measure the vertical and horizontal center of your board—this will be where you attach the center knob. Mark where the other two doorknobs will go, making sure they are evenly spaced out on each side and centered on the board.

4. Drill holes that are slightly larger than your hex bolts at each spot you have marked.

5. Insert your hex bolts from the back of the board and attach the doorknobs from the front.

6. Add a sturdy sawtooth picture hanger to the back.

Colorful Wooden Bunting

Difficulty: Beginner

This adorable wood bunting is a fun home décor piece that doubles as a unique party decoration. Let the wood be the star or add letters to personalize it. You can hang it over a crib in a nursery or keep it on hand as a reusable birthday banner to pull out every year.

Materials

- Scrap wood (pieces at least 4" x 8")
- 100-grit sandpaper
- Paint and chip brush or paintbrush
- Stain and clean rag
- Twine

Tools

- Safety glasses
- Hearing protection
- Tape measure
- Pencil
- Straightedge
- Jigsaw
- Drill and drill bits

Dimensions

Each triangle is 4" wide by 8" long, but you can make it in any size you want. The total length of your bunting will depend on how many triangles you add.

Steps

1. Gather your scrap wood of different paint or stain finishes; you can also paint them later on in step 8. Any wood will work as long as the pieces are large enough to cut triangles from. The final product will look best if all of your wood pieces are close to the same thickness.

2. To create a nice symmetric triangle, draw a straight line for the top edge (you can use the edge of the wood) and mark the bottom point of the triangle—make sure the bottom point is centered halfway between the two top corners. Then, use a straightedge to connect the three corners of the triangle.

3. Cut out your triangles. Once your first triangle is cut, use it as a pattern to trace out the rest of your wood pieces.

4. Once your wooden triangles are cut, use a drill to drill two holes into the top corners of each triangle. Again, once you drill holes in the first triangle, use it as a pattern to mark where the holes on the other pieces should go.

5. Lightly sand the edges of your wooden pieces to remove any rough edges.

6. If you haven't painted your triangles yet, this is a good time. There are numerous different colors and styles you can choose to paint your wood banner. The finishes on this bunting were done using golden oak stain, white paint, light gray paint, dark gray paint, and turquoise paint. Dry-brushing different combinations of the colors onto each piece using a chip brush provides a lovely variety of finishes.

7. The last step is to string your wood pieces on twine by running the twine through the drilled holes. In addition to adding a rustic look, the twine is also helpful in gripping the wood pieces in place, making it very easy to adjust the spacing between triangles if you need.

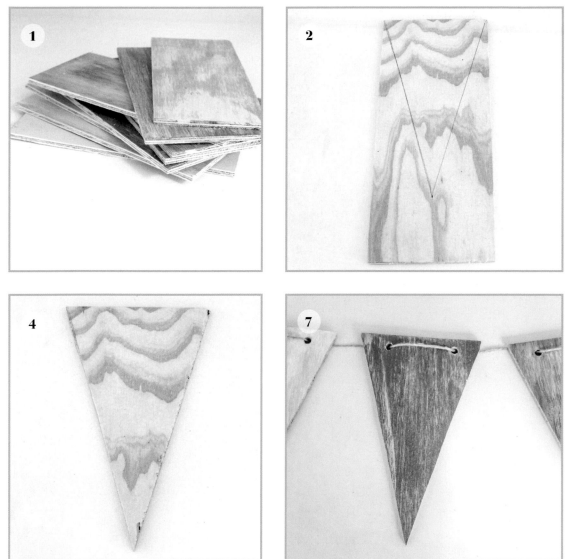

Wooden Boot Tray

Difficulty: Easy

Having a designated spot for dirty boots next to the door can save your floors from unnecessary dirt and grime. This boot tray keeps shoes corralled by the door in a mudroom or entryway, collected in one convenient spot where they are easy to find.

Materials

- Three 1" x 4" x 8' common boards
- 1" x 2" common board
- 100-grit sandpaper
- Wood glue
- Finishing nails
- Stain
- Clean rags and/or brushes
- Waterproofing sealer or exterior paint

Tools

- Safety glasses
- Hearing protection
- Tape measure
- Pencil
- Saw
- Hammer or nail gun

Dimensions

The final boot tray is 4" high, 36" long, and 13.5" wide.

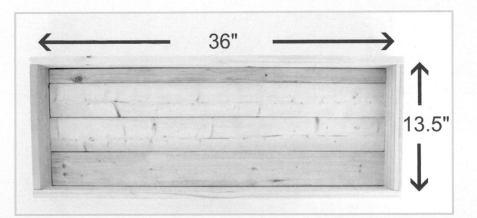

Steps

1. Cut the 1" x 4" boards into two 36" pieces and two 12" pieces. This will form the outer frame. For the bottom of the tray, cut three 34.5"-long 1" x 4" pieces and one 34.5"-long 1" x 2" piece.

2. Sand all of the rough edges from the wood.

3. Lay all four 34.5"-long pieces together on a flat surface to form the bottom of the boot tray. Use wood glue to attach the two 12" pieces to each end. Secure them with a couple of finishing nails into each of the bottom boards.

4. Put the 36" pieces in place to complete the frame.

5. Secure them with wood glue and use finishing nails to attach them to the sides of the frame.

6. Use the paint or stain of your choice and apply with rags or a brush. This boot tray is finished using Minwax provincial stain and Minwax quick-dry polyurethane.

7. It is always a good idea to protect your finish with a good sealer, and especially important for projects like this boot tray. This piece will get a lot of wear and water damage from damp shoes and boots, and so a good sealer will help protect the wood and finish from becoming damaged.

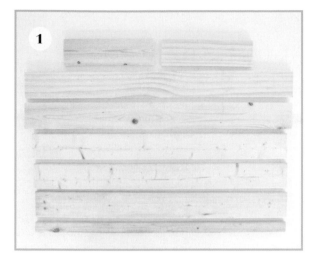

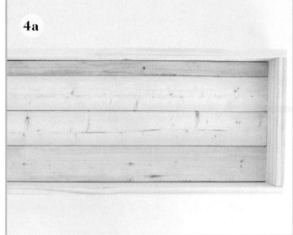

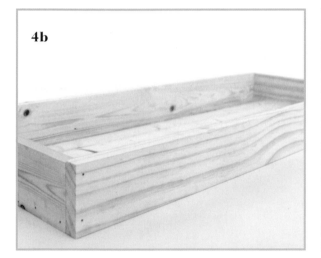

Wooden Arrow Growth Chart

Difficulty: Easy

This cute growth chart is the perfect way to keep track of your growing family. It's also stylish enough to look good in any room in the house. Plus, you can easily pack it up and take it with you anytime you move—which you certainly can't do with the measurements you mark on a doorway!

Materials

- 1" x 12" x 8' pine board
- 100-grit sandpaper
- Paint
- Stain
- Mineral spirits
- Clean rags and/or brushes
- Printout of numbers
- Black oil-based paint marker
- Command picture hanging strips

Tools

- Safety glasses
- Hearing protection
- Tape measure
- Pencil
- Jigsaw

Dimensions

The finished arrow is 6.5' high and 11¼" wide at the widest part of the arrowhead and the arrow's tail. The arrowhead is 14" tall and the tail section is 15" long. The skinny shaft of the arrow is 5" wide.

Steps

1. Begin by drawing an arrow shape (according to the dimensions above) onto the pine board using a pencil and a straight edge. Cut it out with a jigsaw and sand any rough edges smooth.

2. Lean your arrow against a wall to make sure it is straight. If it is a bit crooked, you can trim a small amount off one of the tails until it straightens out.

3. Finish your wooden arrow with any color stain or paint you want. The weathered white finish here is fairly easy, but it does require several steps. First, paint the entire arrow with one coat of the white paint and let it dry. Lightly sand the arrow with 100-grit sandpaper to expose some of the raw wood and wood grain. Use a clean rag to wipe on a coat of a dark stain. Pour a little mineral spirits onto a second clean rag and wipe as much stain as possible off, making sure to use a clean section of the rag each time you wipe it. This will leave you with a perfectly weathered finish.

4. Use a tape measure and a pencil to mark off every 12"-interval from the bottom.

5. Draw your numbers on freehand if you want. But if you don't love your handwriting, use a stencil or print out large numbers in a font you like and do a simple pencil transfer by rubbing pencil all over the back of each number, carefully taping them front-side up onto the arrow where you want them placed, and then tracing over each number with the pencil. When you remove the paper, you'll see a faint pencil outline of the number.

6. Use a black oil-based paint pen to fill in each number and draw on tick marks next to each number at the exact measurement mark. If you would like to soften the look of the black paint, wait until the paint dries and then lightly with 220-grit sandpaper.

7. Be sure to secure your arrow to the wall to prevent it from tipping: command picture hanging strips are the simplest way to do this. They use strong Velcro and do not damage walls when removed. You are ready to start taking measurements.

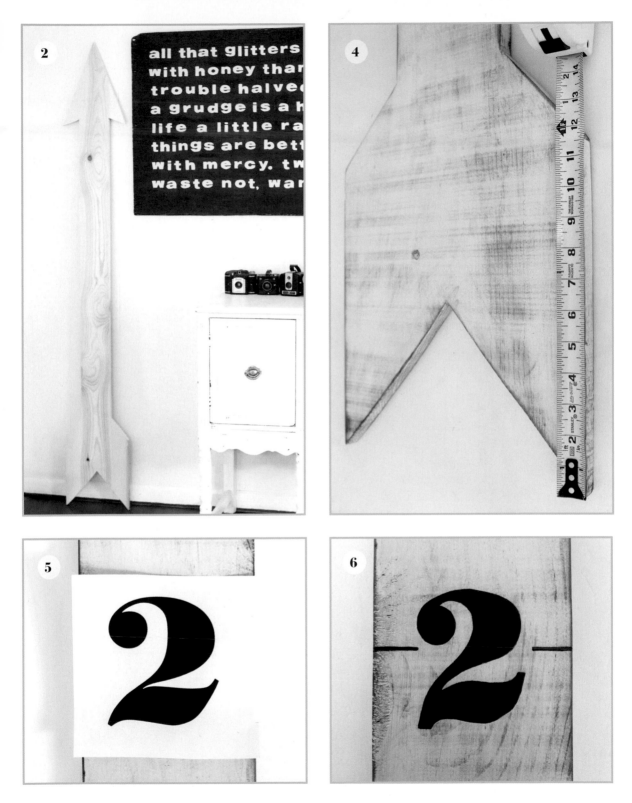

Reclaimed Wood Shelves

Difficulty: Moderate

I don't need any more storage . . . said no one, ever. These shelves are a great way to add more storage to a small space or simply give a blank wall some style. They are easy and inexpensive to make, and they create beautiful open shelving for a kitchen, bathroom, or any other wall.

Materials

- Reclaimed wood or a 1" x 10" common board
- 2" x 2" furring strip
- 1" x 2" pine common board
- 100-grit sandpaper
- Wood glue
- Finishing nails
- White paint
- Dark stain
- Clean rags and/or brushes
- 2½" screws for hanging
- Anchors as needed

Tools

- Safety glasses
- Hearing protection
- Tape measure
- Pencil
- Miter saw
- Hammer
- Drill and drill bits

Dimensions

The shelves shown are 36" wide and 8" deep. The shelf brackets are 7.5" tall and 7.5" deep. This size will work for most shelves, but you can easily adapt these instructions for larger shelves.

Tip

As with most boards, 2" x 2" boards are actually 1.5" by 1.5".

Steps

1. Choose reclaimed wood planks or new boards for the shelves. The wood for the shelves shown here is 8" wide. Cut your shelf boards to the length you want; these shelves are 36" long.

2. To form the shelf brackets, cut a 2" x 2" board to 7.5" (or whatever length you have chosen for your supports, which should be slightly shorter than your shelves so they do not stick out) Cut a second piece to 6" (or 1.5" shorter than the first piece).

3. To make the final side of the shelf brackets, use a miter saw to cut the 1" x 2" board 5.5" long, with a 45-degree angle cut along each side as shown in the photo

4. Sand any rough edges.

5. Use wood glue and finishing nails to connect the three pieces to form the shelf bracket (the side view is shown).

6. Depending on the look you want, you may choose to either paint or stain your shelf supports. The supports here were given a weathered paint look to complement the reclaimed wood shelves. For a similar finish, first paint the shelf brackets white. Then, sand them to reveal some of the raw wood beneath; really concentrate the sanding around the edges and corners. Next, using a clean rag, wipe a dark stain all over the entire bracket. Immediately afterward, use a second clean rag dipped in mineral spirits to wipe away all of the excess stain. After every few wipes, begin with a clean section of the rag. This gives a nice, weathered finish.

7. Predrill holes through your shelf brackets and hang them using sturdy screws.

8. As with all shelves, it is important to screw directly into wall studs or to use strong wall anchors.

9. Firmly attach your shelves to your brackets with wood screws.

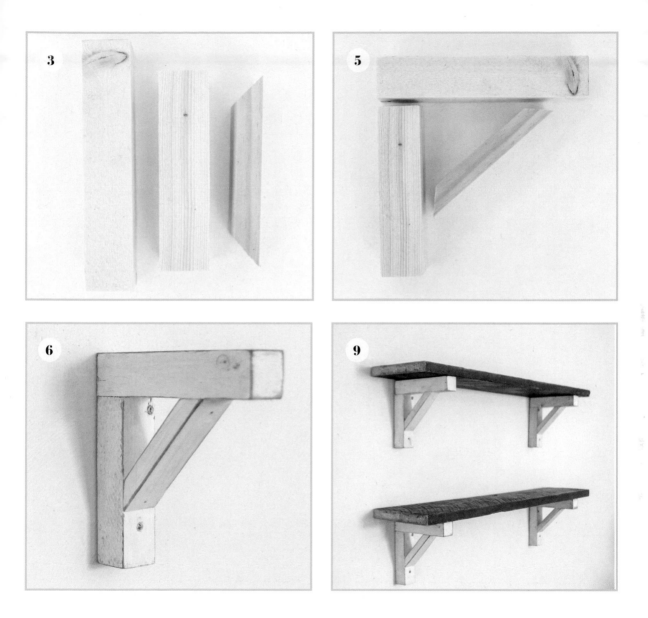

Outdoor Décor

Address Sign with Planter

Difficulty: Moderate

A new address sign will quickly and easily improve your home's curb appeal. This sign displays your house number in a stylish way—and it also features a sweet planter box. Just put your favorite flowers or pretty succulents in the planter to add a bit of color and life to your front door. To keep things extra simple, this entire address sign, including the planter, can be made from just one wood plank.

Materials

- 1" x 4" x 8' common board
- 100-grit sandpaper
- 2 paint stirrers or thin scraps of wood @ 10" long
- ¾" nails or wood screws
- Wood glue
- Finishing nails
- Metal house numbers
- Stain
- Waterproofing sealer
- Paint
- Clean rags and/or brushes

Tools

- Safety glasses
- Hearing protection
- Tape measure
- Pencil
- Saw
- Drill and drill bits
- Hammer or nail gun

Dimensions

The finished address sign is 16" high, 10.5" wide, and 5" deep.

Steps

1. Cut the 1" x 4" x 8' common board into three pieces that are 16" long, one piece that is 10.5" long, two pieces that are 3.5" long, and one piece that is 9" long. Sand any rough edges.

2. Lay the three 16" boards next to each other, facedown, on a flat surface. Make sure the ends line up well. Next, lay the two paint stirrers or any other thin scraps of wood, cut to 10" long, across the back of the three boards. Use ¾" nails or wood screws to attach them to each of the three boards to form a sturdy back that secures them together.

3. Next, build the planter box. Use wood glue and finishing nails to attach the two 3.5" boards to the 10.5" board to form a three-sided box.

4. If you are planning to plant real plants in your planter, use your drill to drill several drainage holes in the 9" piece of wood. Slide it into place as the bottom of the box and attach it to each short end using finishing nails.

5. Attach the planter box to the front of the three-board address sign using finishing nails.

6. Finish your wooden house number with stain and waterproofing sealer or exterior paint. Be sure to finish the inside of the planter box as well to help prevent the wood from becoming damaged by water from the plants. This sign was finished with Minwax Provincial stain and Minwax Polyurethane.

7. Attach your house numbers to the top of the sign with the included screws.

8. Plant whichever small plants you desire, keeping in mind the climate where you live and how much sun or shade your address sign will receive.

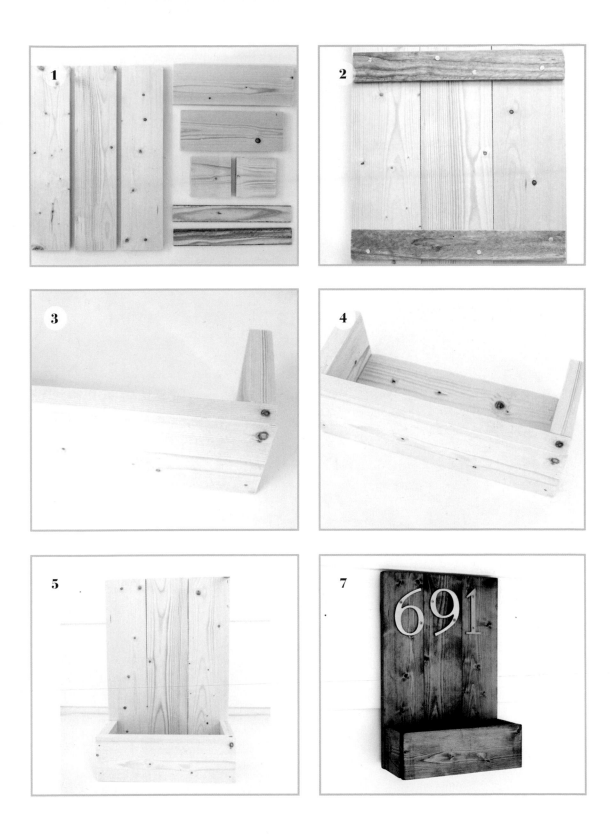

Simple Outdoor Wood Lanterns

Difficulty: Moderate

Lanterns are one of those rare home accessories that will look gorgeous outdoors, next to your front door or alongside your patio furniture. You can even use them for an outdoor wedding! Make one large lantern or build a group in varying sizes to make a stunning centerpiece with big impact. Then, just add candles or a pretty potted plant.

Materials

Wood for large lantern:
- Two ¾" scrap wood @ 9" x 9"
- Five 1" x 1" x 3' square dowels

Wood for small lantern:
- Two ¾" scrap wood @ 7" x 7"
- Three 1" x 1" x 3' square dowels

Other Materials:
- 100-, 150-, and 220-grit sandpaper
- Wood glue
- Finishing nails
- Stain
- Waterproofing sealer
- Clean rags and/or brushes

Dimensions

The larger lantern is 9" square at the base and 20.5" tall. The smaller lantern is 7" square at the base and 15.5" tall. These two sizes will look beautiful together as a pair. If you'd like to make a lantern trio, build an 8" square lantern that is 18" tall.

Tip

Purchase the dowels precut to save some time. If you prefer to save money and make your own dowels, you can cut 1" scrap wood planks into 1" x 1" dowels yourself using a table saw.

Tools

- Safety glasses
- Hearing protection
- Tape measure
- Pencil
- Saw
- Hammer or nail gun

Steps

1. Get the 9"-square and 7"-square scrap wood ready for the large and small lanterns. The rest of the lantern is made using the 1"-square dowels, which are cut into different pieces. For the larger lantern, cut four pieces that are 18" long, 8 pieces that are 7" long, 2 pieces that are 6" long, and two pieces that are 4" long. For the smaller lantern, cut four pieces that are 13" long, eight pieces that are 5" long, two pieces that are 4" long, and two pieces that are 2" long.

2. Sand any rough edges.

3. Lay one of the long pieces—18" for the large lantern and 13" for the small lantern—onto a flat surface and line it up with the corner of the square base—9" square for the large lantern and 7" square for the small lantern—to start building the large and small lanterns respectively. Use wood glue and a finishing nail to attach them together, nailing through the bottom of the base into the long support. Repeat for the other three supports. Be careful not to drip wood glue on the lantern as wood glue will mess up the stained finish.

4. Stand the lantern up and glue four of the 7" pieces (for the large lantern) and 5" pieces (for the small lantern) into place at the base between each support. You may need to cut or sand small bits off these supports to get them to fit exactly in place. Allow the glue to dry.

5. Attach the top of the lantern—9" square for the large lantern and 7" square for the small lantern—to the four long supports with wood glue and nails.

6. Turn the lantern over and attach the other four 7" or 5" pieces in the same way at the base between the four long supports for the large and small lanterns respectively.

7. Allow the glue to dry and then turn the lantern right-side up again. Form a square on top of the lantern using the remaining pieces—the two 6" and two 4" pieces for the large lantern and the two 4" and two 2" pieces for the small lantern. Glue them into place.

8. Before staining the wood, it is a good idea to sand any rough edges smooth. Any of the cut edges that are exposed will absorb a lot of stain and look much darker than the rest of the wood, so to minimize this, use 100-grit sandpaper, followed by 150-grit and 220-grit sandpaper on raw wood edges to get a smooth finish.

9. Finish your lantern with the stain of your choice. These lanterns are finished with one coat of Minwax special walnut, followed by one coat of Minwax dark walnut everywhere except the cut edges.

10. Finish with a good waterproofing sealer, particularly if you plan to use these lanterns outdoors.

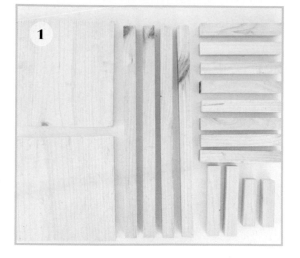

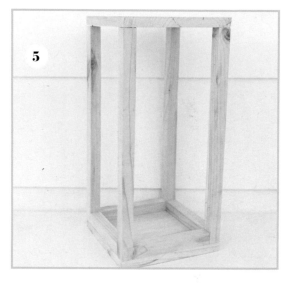

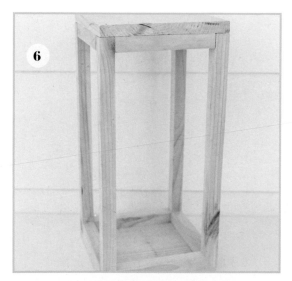

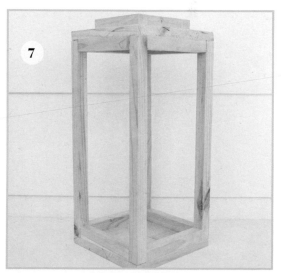

Vertical Wall Planter

Difficulty: Easy

Who says plants can't grow on walls? This adorable vertical planter will bring life to any space, indoors or outdoors. Create a cute vertical garden on a boring fence or plain patio wall; and if you don't have an outdoor space for a garden, plant one right on your apartment wall. Love the feel and aesthetic of plants but can't escape your black thumb? Just add faux plants and you're all set.

Materials

- Three 1" x 4" x 8' pine furring strips, or seven 32" and two 27" strips of pallet wood
- 100-grit sandpaper
- Wood glue
- 1" exterior screws
- 6 metal hooks and the screws they come with
- 2 d-ring picture hangers and picture hanging wire
- Galvanized buckets

Tools

- Safety glasses
- Hearing protection
- Tape measure
- Pencil
- Saw
- Drill and drill bits
- Metal drill bit

Dimensions

The final wall planter is 32" wide and 28" tall.

Tip

Wood pallets are perfect for this project, but there are several other types of wood planks that also work well. Cedar fence pickets are very inexpensive; plus, cedar is a great choice for projects that are going to live outdoors. Simple pine furring strips are also a good, inexpensive option as long as they are sealed against the weather.

Steps

1. Cut seven piece of wood that are 32" long. Cut an additional two pieces that are 27" long. Sand any rough edges.

2. Arrange the seven 32" pieces of wood facedown on a flat surface, leaving around 0.5" of space between each board.

3. Lay the two 27" pieces of wood across them. Predrill holes through each board and use wood glue and wood screws to attach them, making sure to insert two screws through each board.

4. Turn the entire thing over, faceup. Lay out your six metal hooks with 3 hooks centered and evenly spaced from each other across the second board down from the top and another 3 hooks centered and evenly spaced across the fifth board from the top.

5. Predrill holes and then attach the hooks with the screws that came with them.

6. Use a screwdriver to attach two d-rings to the back. These should be attached on either side of the frame approximately one-third of the way down from the top. Angle the d-rings slightly toward the center of the frame.

7. Cut a piece of picture wire twice the width of the frame. Loop the picture wire through each d-ring and twist the two ends firmly together in the middle. Make sure the wire is not so long that it shows above the frame when hanging.

8. If you are planning to use this outdoors, drill several holes into the bottom of each galvanized bucket to allow for drainage. If you want to use this indoors with real plants, add rocks to the bottom of each bucket before adding soil to keep excess water away from the roots. If you are using faux plants, skip this step.

9. Plant your plants in each bucket and hang on the hooks.

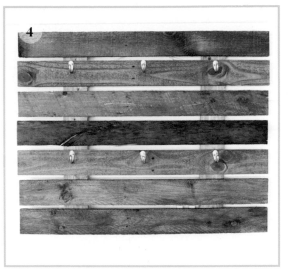

Shaker-Style Wood Shutters

Difficulty: Advanced

Nice shutters can be incredibly expensive, but you can make your own! These DIY wooden shutters are simple, stylish, and major money-savers. Even better—you can easily customize them to perfectly fit your windows, even if they are of unusual sizes. Paint them in your favorite trim color or stain them for a beautiful, natural wood look.

Materials

- 1" x 4" x 8' pine boards
- 1" x 5" x 8' pine boards, or 1" x 6" x 8' pine boards (depending on shutter size)
- 100- and 220-grit sandpaper
- Wood glue
- 1¼" pocket screws
- 1¼" exterior screws
- Exterior paint or stain and waterproofing sealer
- Clean rags and/or brushes

Dimensions

The dimensions of your shutters will depend on the size of your windows. The shutters shown are 13.5" wide and 40" tall.

Tip

Remember, 1" x 4" wood planks are actually 0.75" x 3.5". 1" x 5" wood planks are actually 0.75" x 4.5". And 1" x 6" wood planks are actually 0.75" x 5.5".

Tools

- Safety glasses
- Hearing protection
- Tape measure
- Pencil
- Saw
- Pocket hole jig
- Drill and drill bits

Steps

1. Before you begin, determine what size you want to make your shutters. To find the correct height for your shutters, measure the height of your window. The shutters shown are each 13.5" wide, a size that works well for smaller windows, and were made using three 1" x 5" planks. If you are making shutters for larger windows, for example, one that is 16.5" wide, you might prefer to use three 1" x 6" planks. The steps here detail how to make one shutter; simply repeat the process for the second shutter to make a pair.

2. Cut two pieces of 1" x 4" wood to the height of your window you measured earlier.

3. Cut three 1" x 5" or 1" x 6" wood planks to the height of your window you measured earlier.

4. Cut three 1" x 4" cross pieces for each shutter. These are the three horizontal pieces for the shutter. The dimensions for these pieces should equal the width of one shutter minus 7". If you are making 13.5" shutters, these will be 6.5"; if you are making 16.5" shutters, these will be 9.5".

5. The 1" x 4" pieces from steps 2 and 4 will form the front face of the shutter. Turn the three shorter pieces facedown and drill pocket holes with a pocket hole jig as shown in the photo.

6. Sand any rough edges smooth using 100-grit sandpaper.

7. Use wood glue and 1¼" pocket screws to attach these pieces together for the front frame.

8. Place the front face of the shutter facedown on a flat surface. Lay the three 1" x 5" or 1" x 6" boards you cut on top of this. Use wood glue to attach these.

9. Predrill holes from the back through the frame and then use exterior screws to attach the three boards to the front frame.

10. Sand the entire shutter lightly with 220-grit sandpaper to prepare it for finishing. Finish with exterior paint or stain and waterproofing sealer.

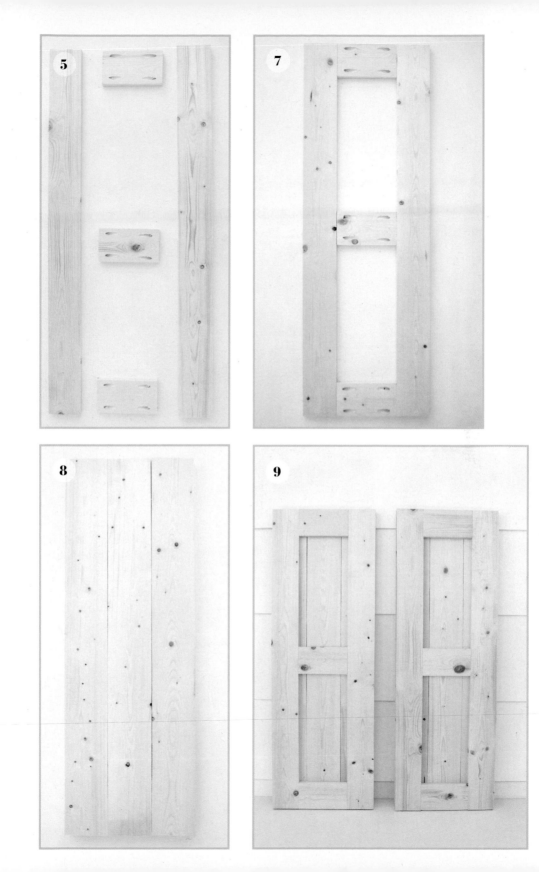

Wooden Planter Box

Difficulty: Advanced

A sturdy wooden planter box is the perfect way to highlight a favorite plant. Large store-bought planters may be very expensive, but this version costs less than fifteen dollars to make. Beautifully weathered, this will look wonderful in your yard or patio or as a pair flanking your front door.

Materials

- Three 1" x 4" x 8' furring strips
- 2" x 2" x 8' pine board
- 1¼" coarse pocket hole screws
- Stain and waterproofing sealer or exterior paint
- Clean rags and/or brushes

Tools

- Safety glasses
- Hearing protection
- Tape measure
- Pencil
- Miter saw
- Pocket hole jig
- Drill

Dimensions

The final planter is 19" high, 17.5" wide at the top, and 14" wide at the bottom.

Steps

1. Each side of the planter contains five 1" x 4" planks cut at a 5-degree angle on each end. Set your miter saw to cut 5-degree cuts. Cut the top plank as shown with a 5-degree angle at each end. The length of the top plank is 14.5".

2. Use this top board to determine the length of the next board. Measure the bottom edge of the top board and cut the top edge of the second board to that same length. Continue measuring this way until all five boards are cut.

3. Use these boards as a pattern to cut the boards for the other three sides of the planter box.

4. The 2" x 2" boards will be the corner supports. Cut the top of the first support at a 5-degree angle with your miter saw, with a length of about 19" long, and making a parallel 5-degree angle cut along the bottom.

5. Use a pocket hole jig to drill four pocket holes on the back of each plank, two along each short end.

6. Now, assemble the first side of the planter. The corner supports are 1.5" thick while the plank sides are ¾" thick. When assembling the planter, the back edge of the planter sides should line up with the back edge of the corner supports. Since they are two different thicknesses, you need to use scrap wood to help align the boards while they are being assembled. Lay a few of the cut pieces of 1" x 4" wood on a flat surface. These planks will act as spacers to raise the planter sides to the same level as the thicker corner supports correctly.

7. Arrange the planks for one side of the planter facedown on top of the spacers. Make sure that the top of the corner supports is flush with the top of the first wood plank. Use a drill and pocket screws to attach the planks to the two corner supports on either side using the pocket holes. This creates the first side.

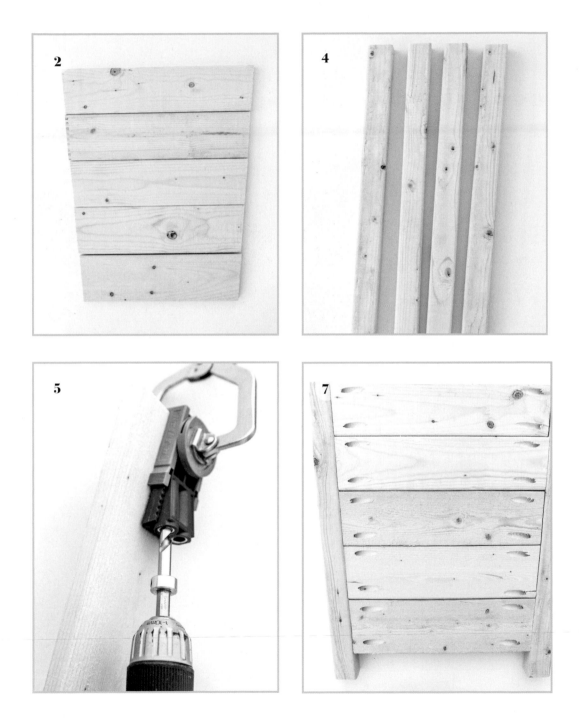

8. Lay out the planks for a second side and attach them to one of the supports from the first side, remembering to line up the top plank and use spacers below the planks to keep them aligned correctly with the corner supports.

9. Add the final two sides in the same manner.

10. Whatever finish you choose for your planter box, make sure it is water resistant. If you choose to use paint, use a good exterior paint. To achieve this weathered gray finish, I used a clean rag to apply a coat of Rustoleum Weathering Accelerator followed by a coat of Varathane sunbleached stain. I finished with a water-resistant sealer.

11. The final step is to add your plant or tree. You can simply set your plant in its inexpensive plastic pot directly into the planter. If the pot is large enough, the angle of the sides will hold it in place. If it needs extra support, you can cut a few scraps of wood and wedge them in at the correct height for your pot.

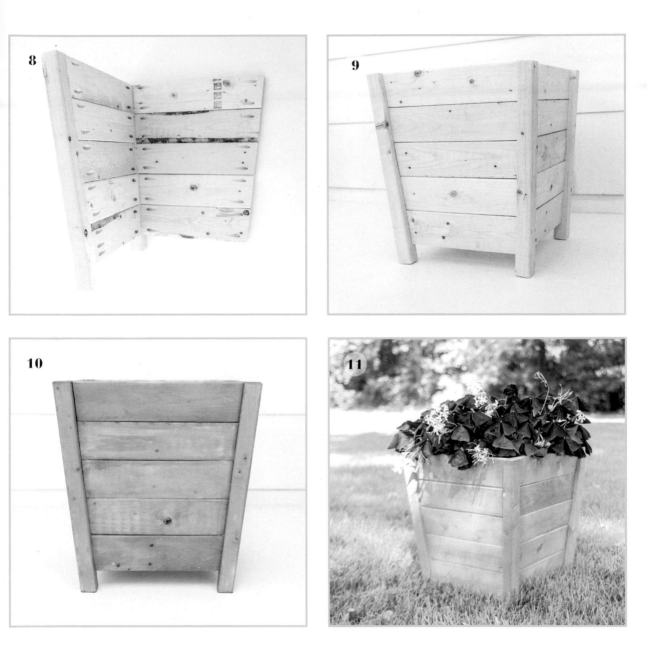

Indoor/Outdoor X Bench

Difficulty: Advanced

This classic bench works beautifully both indoors and outdoors. Made of humble 2" x 4" planks, this bench costs less than twenty dollars to make and is very sturdy. The slat top and water-resistant finish make it perfect for your garden or porch, but it also looks gorgeous at the foot of a bed, in an entryway, or paired with a farmhouse table (page 161).

Materials

- Four 2" x 4" x 8' wood boards
- 100- and 220-grit sandpaper
- Wood glue
- 2" wood screws
- 2" x 2" x 8' wood board
- 2.5" pocket screws
- Finishing nails
- Paint, stain, and sealer
- Clean rags and/or brushes

Tools

- Safety glasses
- Hearing protection
- Tape measure
- Pencil
- Miter saw
- Drill and drill bits
- Pocket hole jig
- Hammer or nail gun

Dimensions

The finished bench is 4' long, 14" wide, and 18" high.

Steps

1. To construct the X legs, position a 2" x 4" board with the narrow 2" side facing up. Cut two pieces that are 16" long, with parallel 30-degree angles at each end, as shown in the photo. These will form the longs sides of each X.

2. Cut four pieces of 2" x 4" board that are 8" long, with a 30-degree angle at each end as shown in the photo.

3. Cut four pieces of 2" x 4" board that are 13" long. These will be the top and bottom supports for each X leg.

4. To add extra detail, turn each 13"-long board on its side and measure 1" from the end of the board. Make a 40-degree miter cut at the 1" mark toward the end of the board. Repeat on the opposite end. This gives a nice angled edge.

5. Sand all of the rough edges with 100-grit sandpaper.

6. Use wood glue and 2" screws to build the legs. Screw the long side of the X and the first 8" piece to the base by screwing two screws through the base into each side of the X. Screw two more screws through the long side of the X into the top of the shorter end.

7. Attach the final 8" piece of the X and the top. Line everything up and then screw through the top into both parts of the X. Finally, screw straight through the long side of the X into the final short side.

8. Repeat for the second leg.

9. Cut the 2" x 2" board 36" long. This will form the support between the two legs. Use your pocket hole jig to drill one pocket hole in each end of this support.

10. Cut the remaining 2" x 4" boards into four 48" pieces. These will form the bench top.

11. Lay out your 48" 2" x 4" planks that will form the top of your bench on a flat surface, facedown. Leave a small gap between each board for water drainage, particularly if you plan to use this bench outdoors. Nickels work perfectly as spacers.

12. Set the legs in place on top of the upside-down bench top. Position the 2" x 2" support between the two legs in the middle of the X, with the pocket holes facing up. Once the bench is flipped right-side up, these pocket holes will be on the bottom. Attach the 2" x 2" supports to the center of each X using 2.5" pocket screws in each pocket hole.

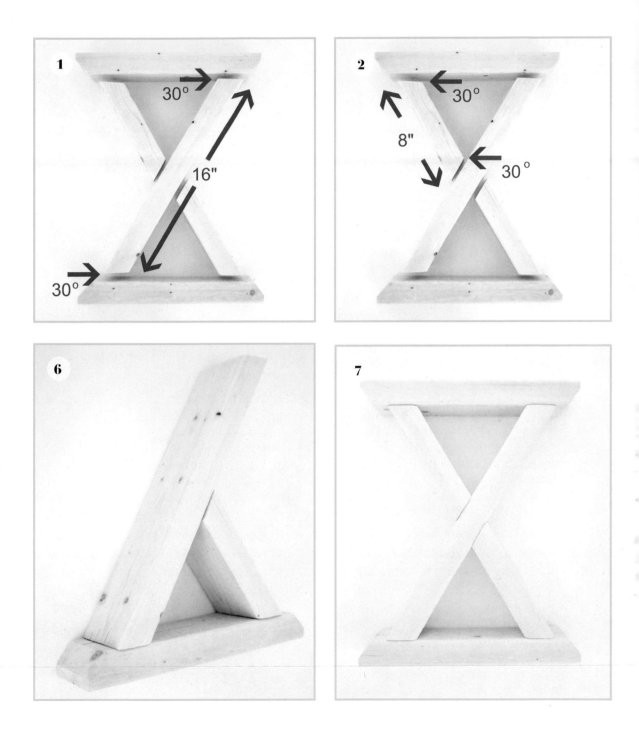

13. Make sure the legs are centered across the planks and are an equal distance from each end of the bench top. Each leg should be around 2.5" from the end of the bench top. Drill two holes through the end of each leg into the top boards and attach them with 2.5" screws. This will secure the two outer boards of the top. The two inner boards cannot be attached in this manner because of the position of the X legs, so they will be secured using nails.

14. Turn the bench over. Lay out the remaining two 2" x 4" boards on the top, using the nickels or quarters as spacers again to keep them spaced evenly. Use finishing nails to attach each board to the legs.

15. To finish, you may prefer to paint the whole thing, stain it, or do a two-tone look like the bench shown. If you choose to stain your bench, it's a good idea to sand the wood lightly with 220-grit sandpaper first to prepare it for stain. This bench was stained using Rustoleum Kona Stain and sealed with General Finishes High Performance Flat Topcoat. The bottom was painted using white exterior paint.

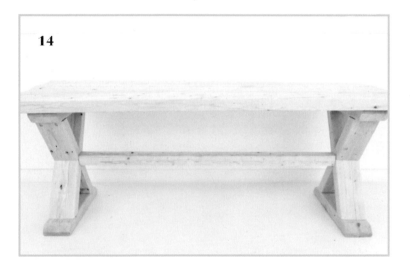

Statement-Making Pieces

Weathered Wood Plank Wall

Difficulty: Easy

If your home doesn't come with any interesting architecture to speak of, you might want to consider adding your own texture and interest to bland walls. This weathered plank wall has the gorgeous look of reclaimed wood—without the stress of looking for actual reclaimed wood. Even better, it is incredibly affordable and made using inexpensive plywood. The beautiful finishes are created using paints and stains.

Materials

- ¼" plywood cut into 4", 6", and 8" planks (2 sheets of 4' x 8' plywood for an 8' wall.)
- Various chalk paints or acrylic craft paints
- Chip brush or paint brush
- Paper towel (optional)
- Stain and clean rag
- Finishing nails
- Electrical outlet spacers (optional)

Tools

- Safety glasses
- Hearing protection
- Tape measure
- Pencil
- Table saw or circular saw, for cutting plywood into strips
- Miter saw or circular saw, for cutting planks to length
- Stud finder
- Level
- Hammer or nail gun
- Jigsaw

Dimensions

Each 4' x 8' sheet of plywood will cover 32 square feet of wall. If you have typical 8' ceilings, two sheets of plywood will cover an 8' section of wall.

Steps

1. When choosing wood for this project, look for plywood with a lot of texture and visible wood grain. You can have your plywood cut into strips at the store or you can use a table saw or circular saw to cut it yourself. Cut each sheet of plywood into four 6" strips, two 8" strips, and two 4" strips.

2. Once your planks are cut, stain and paint them; it is so much easier to paint each plank before installing them. For this small entryway wall, I simply installed one plank per row. If you are planking a longer wall, you will need more than one strip of wood in each row. You can either paint all of the wood in each row in the same way or mix up the finishes for a more eclectic look.

3. To achieve this unique textured, weathered finish reminiscent of reclaimed wood, my go-to technique is dry-brushing using a chip brush or any other paintbrush. Put a very small amount of paint on your brush and then wipe as much paint off as possible on the lip of the paint can. To remove even more paint, you can wipe your brush on a paper towel several times. You want your brush to be as dry as possible while still having a bit of paint on it. Next, lightly brush your paint across the board. Because dry-brushing applies very little paint, you can add multiple colors without having to wait for the paint to dry in between. This wall was created using golden oak stain and white, light gray, dark gray, and aqua paint. A chalk paint or even an acrylic craft paint with a matte finish will work best. Dry-brushing various combinations of just a few different colors can give a variety of different finishes.

4. Once everything is painted, it is time to install the wall. If your wall ends at an exposed corner like in this entryway, cut one of your 4" plywood strips in half to make two 2" strips. Hang one of these thin strips vertically at the edge of the wall where your plank wall will be. This will act as a clean edge for the plank wall.

5. Lay your planks out on the floor to get an idea of how you want to arrange the various finishes.

6. Use a stud finder to mark where the studs are in the wall. Trim your planks to the correct length and then, starting immediately above the base molding, hang them one by one. Use a level to check each board before attaching it. Because plywood is so light, simply nail them to the wall with a finishing nail in each stud. This will be plenty secure, and you will be able to easily remove them in the future.

7. As you hang the planks, use a few pennies or nickels between each board to keep the spacing between boards even.

8. You will need to use a jigsaw to cut holes wherever there are outlets and light switches. You may also have to make special cuts to fit the plank wall around door frames and windows. Once your plank wall is finished, you may need to use a few spacers to ensure that your outlets and switches are flush with the new wall.

9. Trim the final wood planks to fit flush against the ceiling.

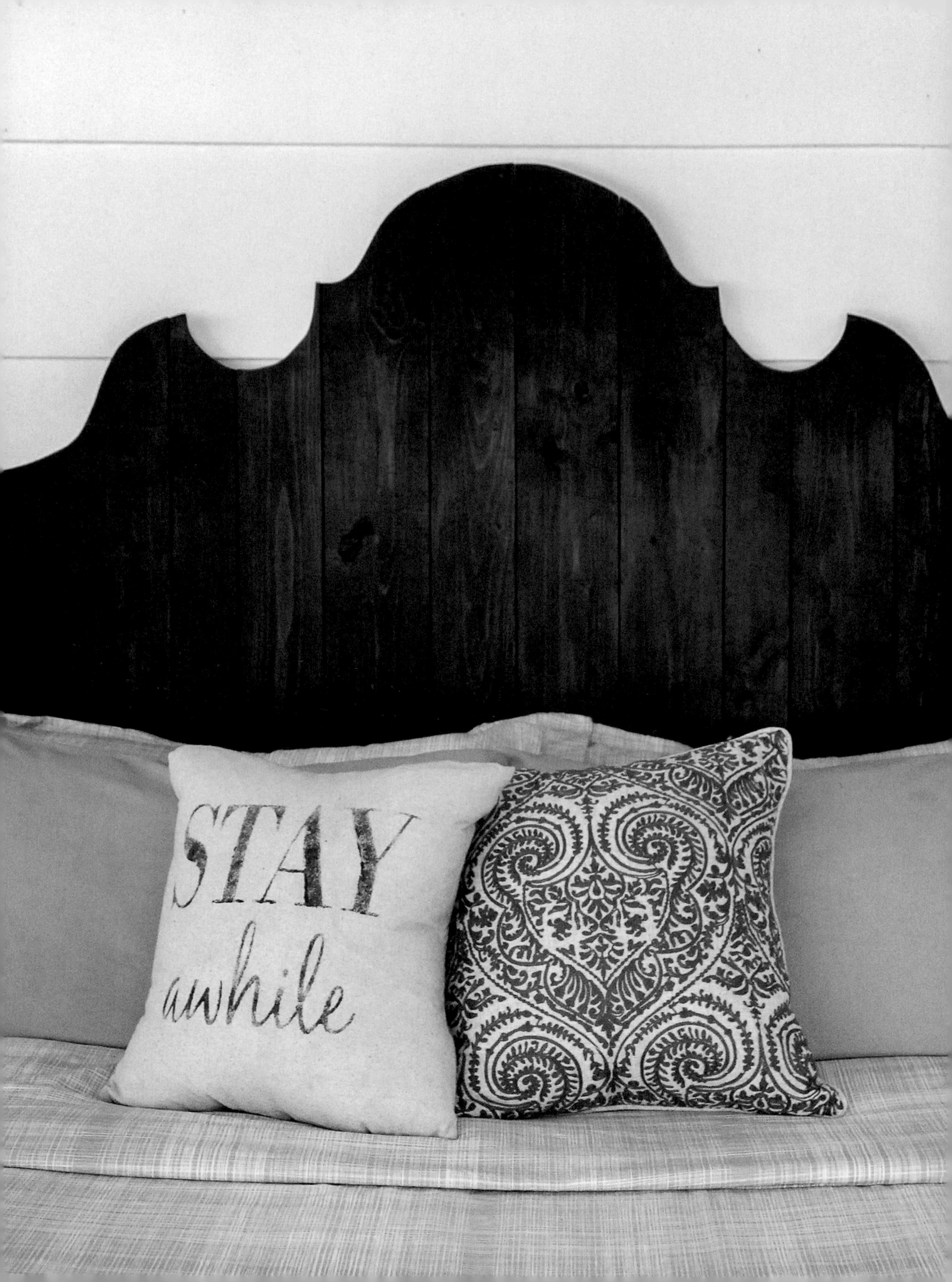
STAY
awhile

Curvy Wooden Headboard

Difficulty: Moderate

Headboards will easily create a beautiful focal point in a "blah" bedroom. This curvy wood plank headboard strikes the perfect balance between feminine and masculine, rustic and modern. It will look lovely in your master bedroom, a guest room, or even behind a pair of twin beds in a child's bedroom. This version is sized for a queen bed, but the measurements can easily be adjusted to work for any size.

Materials

- Three 1" x 4" x 8' common board
- 1" x 5" x 8' common board
- Three 1" x 6" x 8' common board
- Two 1" x 5" x 6' common boards, for the two ends of the headboard
- Wrapping paper, butcher paper, or other large paper, to make a pattern
- 100- and 220-grit sandpaper
- Stain and sealer
- Clean rags and/or brushes
- Two 1" x 4" x 8' furring strip
- Wood glue
- 1¼" wood screws
- French cleat hardware, for attaching the headboard to the wall (optional)

Tools

- Safety glasses
- Hearing protection
- Tape measure
- Pencil
- Saw
- Jigsaw
- Palm sander (optional)
- Drill and drill bits

Dimensions

This queen size headboard is 63" wide and 68" high at the tallest point. To make a headboard for a different size bed, simply adjust the width.

Tip

This curvy headboard will also look great in a lighter, weathered stain or painted with an old chippy paint look.

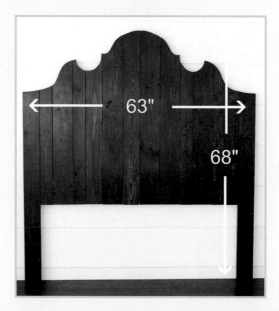

Steps

1. Start by cutting the 1" x 4" x 8', 1" x 5" x 8', and 1" x 6" x 8' boards in half to make 4' boards. Arrange the boards in a random pattern with the two 1" x 5" x 6' boards on each end.

2. Cut a large piece of wrapping paper or other large paper into 63" or the width of the headboard. This will form the pattern for your headboard design. It is easier to draw and adjust a pattern on paper until it is just right than it is to draw a pattern directly onto the wood.

3. Fold the paper in half and draw out the shape you would like for your headboard. Cut it out.

4. Unfold the pattern and trace it onto your wood planks.

5. Use a pencil to label the back of each plank with a number, numbering them from left to right. This will make it easier to assemble the headboard together at the end.

6. Use a jigsaw to cut out the shape you drew, one plank at a time.

7. Sand the rough edges using 100-grit sandpaper Also lightly sand each of the edges along the front face of each board so they are slightly more rounded. This will give the wood a more rustic look and accentuate the fact that they are separate planks. You may choose to use a palm sander so this goes a bit faster, but sanding by hand is also fine.

8. Lightly sand the front of each plank using 220-grit sandpaper to prepare for stain.

9. Now, stain or paint your planks. It is easier to get the stain into the tiny grooves between each plank before they are attached together. The finish shown is Rustoleum Kona Stain followed by General Finishes High Performance Topcoat in Flat. This is a great stain for getting a dark, even finish on inexpensive pine boards. The General Finishes High Performance Topcoat is great for rustic projects because it has only the slightest hint of sheen.

10. Once the stain has dried, arrange the planks back in order, facedown. Cut two 1" x 4" x 8' strips of pine furring to 60" long, or a few inches less than the width of the headboard.

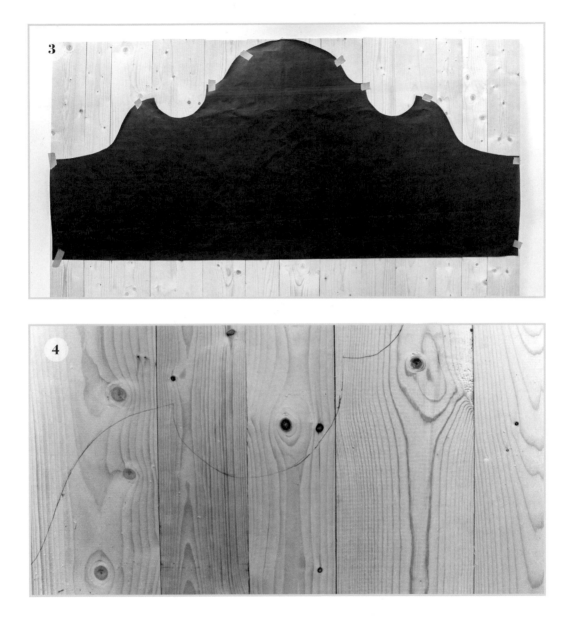

11. Lay the two strips across the planks on the back of the headboard, and use wood glue to attach it. Predrill holes attaching each plank of the headboard to each of the two strips. Attach the planks to the two strips using 1¼" wood screws.

12. Be sure to secure your headboard to the wall before using it. A common method is using a sturdy French cleat. Use the included screws to attach one side to the headboard and the other side to the wall. The two pieces interlock securely when you slide your headboard into place.

11

12

Farmhouse Bench

Difficulty: Moderate

You would never guess this sweet little bench isn't a true antique. Building your own bench means no waiting around to find the perfect vintage piece. Modeled after old country benches, the curvy legs and distressed paint job make it stand out. This piece will look right at home on a porch, in an entryway, at a table, or even at the foot of a bed.

Materials

- 1" x 12" pine board, for the legs
- Wrapping paper, butcher paper, or any large paper, to make a pattern
- Tape
- 100- and 220-grit sandpaper
- 1" x 5" x 8' pine plank
- 1¼" pocket screws
- 1" x 4" x 4' pine plank
- Wood glue
- Finishing nails
- Paint or stain
- Matte sealer
- Clean rags and/or brushes

Dimensions

The final bench is 31" long, 13.5" wide, and 18" tall. You can easily make your bench longer if you prefer.

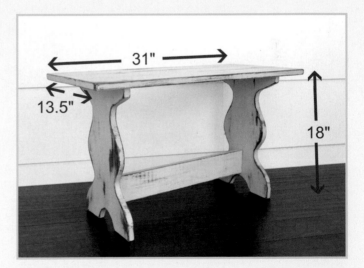

Tools

- Safety glasses
- Hearing protection
- Tape measure
- Pencil
- Saw
- Jigsaw
- Pocket hole jig
- Sander (optional)
- Hammer or nail gun

Steps

1. Cut the 1" x 12" board into two 17" pieces. These will be the two legs.

2. Cut a piece of wrapping paper or any other large paper to the same size as one of the legs. Fold the paper in half lengthwise and draw the shape you want for the legs onto the paper. Cut it out. When you unfold the paper, you will have a pattern with two matching sides.

3. Tape the pattern to each piece of wood and trace it with a pencil.

4. Use a jigsaw to cut out the legs. Sand each edge with 100-grit sandpaper to remove any roughness and smooth the sharp corners and edges so it looks aged.

5. Cut the 1" x 5" x 8' board into three pieces that are 31" long. These pieces will form the top.

6. Use your pocket hole jig to add five pocket holes along the long edge of two of the 1" x 5" x 31" boards. Be sure to set the depth collar on your drill bit and the jig placement to the correct positions for ¾"-thick wood before beginning. It is recommended to add a pocket hole every 6" along the joint.

7. Line up the three top boards and attach them using a 1¼" pocket screw in each pocket hole.

8. Sand the bench top with 100-grit sandpaper, followed by 220-grit sandpaper, smoothing all of the corners and edges.

9. Cut the 1" x 4" x 4' plank to 21.5" long to make the leg support. Sand the edges with 100-grit sandpaper to smooth them.

10. Drill two pocket holes along the top edge of each bench leg.

11. Place the bench top upside down on a flat surface. Position the legs upside down above the top, using the 1" x 4" support as a spacer. Each leg will be approximately 4" from the ends of the bench top. Make sure to center the first leg before attaching it. Add wood glue to the top of the bench leg and attach it to the bench top using a pocket screw in each pocket hole. It is helpful to have an extra pair of hands while doing this.

12. Attach the second leg the same way.

13. Add wood glue to each end of the 1" x 4" support. Hold it in place approximately three inches from the bottom of the legs and hammer a couple of finishing nails through each leg into the support.

14. You can finish the bench however you choose. This beautiful vintage paint finish began with a coat of Minwax Dark Walnut Stain.

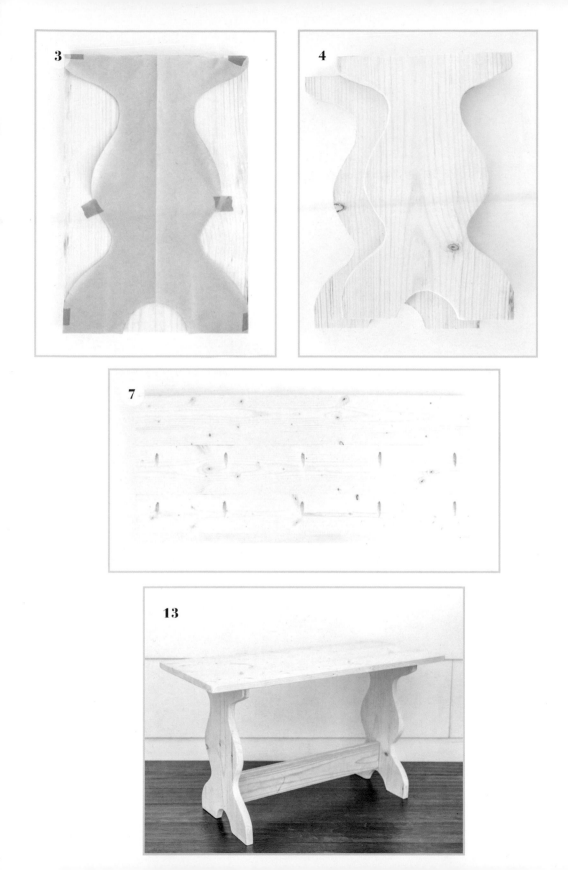

15. Once the stain was completely dry, it was painted with American Décor Chalky Paint in the color Vintage.

16. Then, it was sanded to reveal the dark finish beneath.

17. Finally, it was sealed with General Finishes Flat Out Flat Topcoat.

Removable Herringbone Tabletop

Difficulty: Advanced

The tables in our homes can take a real beating from everyday wear and tear. This removable tabletop, which is basically a slipcover for your table, fits neatly over the original top to create a fresh, new surface. It's also a great solution when you have a table that is no longer your style or when you want to be able to switch back and forth between your old beat-up table, fit for homework and crafts, and something more stylish that can be on display the rest of the time.

Materials

- An old table with sturdy legs (a square or rectangular table)
- ¼" plywood (cut to same size as the old tabletop)
- 1" x 4" x 8' common boards (number of boards depends on the size of the table; 6 boards were used for this table)
- 100- and 220-grit sandpaper
- Wood glue
- Painter's tape
- 1" x 2" or 1" x 3" wood planks (depending on the thickness of the old tabletop)
- Finishing nails
- Stain, paint, or sealer
- Clean rags, chip brush, and/or brushes

Tools

- Safety glasses
- Hearing protection
- Tape measure
- Pencil
- Saw
- Miter saw
- Carpenter's square
- Hammer or nail gun

Dimensions

The dimensions of your tabletop depend on the size of the table you are using. This tabletop is 31" wide and 49.5" long.

Tip

Keep in mind that that 1" x 2" boards are actually ¾" x 1.5", 1" x 3" boards are actually ¾" x 2.5", and 1" x 4" boards are actually ¾" x 3.5".

Steps

1. Measure the top of your old table. Cut your ¼" plywood to the same width and length as your old tabletop.

2. Use a straight edge to draw a line down the center of the plywood lengthwise.

3. The 1" x 4" pine boards will form the herringbone tabletop. Cut one end of the first board at a 45-degree angle using a miter saw. Lay the angled cut of the board along the center line of the short side of the table, making sure there is a 45-degree angle between the table edge and the plank. Use a carpenter's square to ensure it is laid at exactly a 45-degree angle. These first few boards are the foundation for the entire pattern; if they are placed correctly, laying the rest of the wood will be much easier.

4. Use a pencil to mark where the second cut to remove the excess board needs to be by tracing along the edge of the plywood on the underside of the 1" x 4" board. Cut this with your miter saw and sand any rough edges with 100-grit sandpaper.

5. Glue this piece into place.

6. Repeat on the opposite side and then continue to cut and lay wood planks until they reach the other end of the plywood. It helps to use painter's tape to hold the pieces in place until the glue fully dries. It's also important to measure each piece individually before cutting as a slight error can throw off the whole pattern.

7. Once you have completed the majority of the pattern, go back and fill in the corners with shorter pieces of wood.

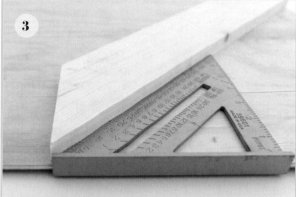

8. Next, make a frame around the entire top. This frame extends down to cover the old tabletop and hold the new tabletop in place. Place your herringbone top on top of your old table and measure the thickness of the two tops combined. The frame around your new tabletop needs to be at least this thick. If your old tabletop is fairly thin, you can use 1" x 2" boards to form this frame; if it is thicker, you may need to use 1" x 3" boards.

9. The tabletop frame will have mitered corners to give a nice, clean edge. Cut a 45-degree angle at one end of your first board. Line this board up with your tabletop and mark the placement for the second cut. Each 45-degree angle will begin at the corner of the tabletop and angle out. Cut the frame pieces for the other three sides in the same manner. Attach it to your herringbone tabletop using wood glue and finishing nails.

10. Continue adding trim on the other three sides of the tabletop.

11. Finish your tabletop however you wish. If you plan to stain your tabletop, it's a good idea to lightly sand it with 220-grit sandpaper to prepare the wood for stain. This finish is Minwax Special Walnut Stain followed by lightly dry-brushed General Finishes Milk Paint in the color Driftwood. The table is sealed with General Finishes High Performance Flat Topcoat.

12. Your new tabletop should fit perfectly over the old one for display at all times. Need to use the old table for messy craft projects? Simply remove the new tabletop.

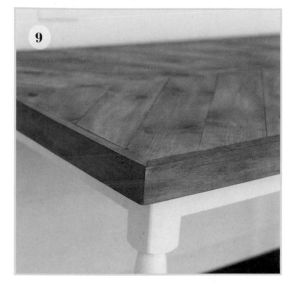

Reclaimed Wood Barn Door

Difficulty: Moderate

This isn't a traditional barn door; it is a truly one-of-a-kind art piece for your home that highlights just how beautiful reclaimed wood can be. Building a door sounds intimidating, but this sliding barn door is actually a very easy project. Don't need a sliding door? This same piece would make a gorgeous headboard; you can also pair it with hairpin legs to make an amazing table.

Materials

- ¾" plywood, cut to the size of door
- ¾" reclaimed wood, pallet wood, or other rustic wood planks
- Paints and stains
- Clean rags and/or brushes
- 100-grit sandpaper
- Wood glue
- Finishing nails
- 2 pieces of 1.5" lattice wood, cut to the height of the door
- Matte sealer
- Sliding barn door hardware

Tools

- Safety glasses
- Hearing protection
- Tape measure
- Pencil
- Table saw, for cutting plywood
- Saw, for cutting planks to size
- Hammer or nail gun

Dimensions

The door shown is 36" by 84". Be sure to measure your own space to get the measurements your need. Remember: you want a sliding door to be slightly larger than the door opening.

Tip

If you aren't sure where to find reclaimed wood, see page 2.

Steps

1. Cut the ¾" plywood to the size of your door (36" x 84" here). You can also have this cut at the hardware store when you buy it.

2. Gather various types of reclaimed wood. It helps if the wood is all the same thickness—¾" thick is a good size. If you need to mix in some new wood planks, look for boards that are straight but that have lots of texture and knotholes.

3. Start arranging the wood planks on top of the plywood. Try to vary the widths of the boards and the finishes. You can choose to do one long plank per row or combine a few shorter boards to make a single row.

4. Once you have an idea of your board arrangement, mark where each board needs to be cut with a pencil and cut them. Sand any rough edges.

5. Even if you mix in plain wood boards, remember that you can use different stains and paints to achieve all kinds of effects. Pictures 5a and 5b are of the exact same section of the door—the second photo was shot after adding different brown and gray wood stains and dry brushing a few shades of gray and white paint.

6. Once your boards look the way you want, use wood glue to glue them to the plywood.

7. Allow the glue to dry and then use a nail gun or hammer to add a small finishing nail to each corner of each board. This will ensure that they stay firmly in place.

8. To finish off the sides, cut two pieces of thin 1.5"-wide lattice wood to the height of your door and stain them in the color of your choice. This door is stained Minwax Special Walnut. Nail them along each side of the door. You can also add lattice trim to the top and bottom of your door if you wish, but those rough edges won't be seen so it isn't necessary.

3

5a

5b

8

9. Stain the back of the door the same stain color you used on the lattice trim.

10. Use a matte sealer to seal the entire door. This will seal in any old, chipping paint and protect the finishes.

11. Hang the door using sliding barn door hardware.

11

Rustic Farmhouse Dining Table

Difficulty: Advanced

This table is the perfect statement piece for any rustic, farmhouse-style space. It works equally well outdoors, on a porch, or in a dining room. You can pair your table with a set of farmhouse chairs, a pair of matching benches (see page 121), or a combination of the two.

Materials

- Three 4" x 4" x 8' boards
- 100-grit sandpaper
- Wood glue
- 2½" wood screws
- Two 2" x 4" x 8' pine boards
- 5.5' reclaimed wood plank, or four 1" x 10" x 6" wood planks
- 1¼" or 1½" pocket screws, depending on the thickness of the wood for your tabletop
- 2" wood screws
- 2½" pocket screws
- Stain or paint and sealer
- Clean rags and/or brushes

Tools

- Safety glasses
- Hearing protection
- Tape measure
- Pencil
- Miter saw
- Circular saw
- Wood chisel
- Drill and drill bits
- Pocket hole jig

Dimensions

The finished table is 38" wide, 66" long, and 29.5" high. Depending on the exact width of the wood you use to make your tabletop, the width of your table may be slightly more or less than 38". The measurements for legs used in the instructions should work for a tabletop between 36" and 44" wide.

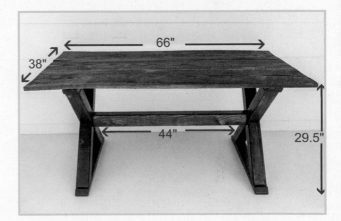

Tip

remember that 4" x 4" boards are actually 3.5" wide.

Steps

1. To construct the X legs, cut two of the 4" x 4" x 8' boards into four pieces that are 36.5" long each, with parallel 45-degree angle cuts on each end. Sand any rough edges. (The photo shows only two pieces.)

2. To form the X legs, you are going to create a lap joint with these two pieces of wood. This is a very strong joint that will ensure that the table is sturdy and can support weight well. Lay your wood down as it appears in the photo accompanying step 1. Measure 18" from one end of the wood. Mark a straight line perpendicular to the board. Repeat on the other side. There should be 3.5" between the two lines.

3. Set your circular saw blade to 1¾". The saw will be cutting halfway through each board, about 1¾" deep. Carefully cut the two lines you drew in the center of your wood. Then, make many parallel cuts close together between those two cuts, also halfway through the wood.

4. Use a wood chisel to knock out all of the slivers of wood from this section.

5. Repeat for the other three legs. Sand any rough edges.

6. Fit two of the legs together to form a tight X. If they don't quite fit, you may need to cut a bit more to make a large enough space. Attach them with wood glue. Predrill holes and use 2.5" screws to connect them. Repeat for the other leg.

7. Cut four pieces of 2" x 4" boards to 35" long each. These will be the top and bottom supports for each X leg.

8. To add extra detail, turn each 2" x 4" x 35" board on its side and measure 1" from the end of the board. Make a 45-degree miter cut at the 1" mark toward the end of the board. This gives it a nice angled edge. Repeat on the other end of the board.

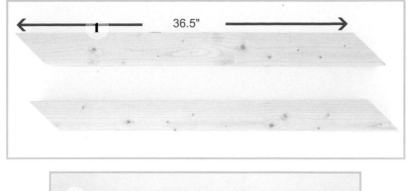

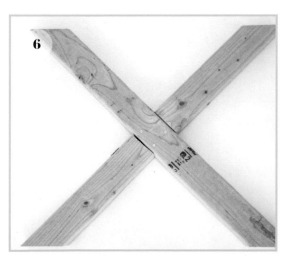

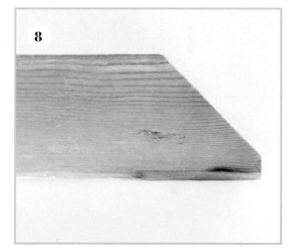

9. Sand any rough edges.

10. Center one of these supports on top of one of your X legs. Attach it with wood glue and 2.5" screws. Attach the other to the bottom of the X legs in the same way.

11. Repeat for second X legs.

12. To make the plank tabletop, cut each of your reclaimed wood planks to 66" long with your circular saw. If using reclaimed wood, lay out your boards first to see how they look and choose the flattest, straightest boards. Sand any roughness from the cut edges.

13. Lay the boards for the table top upside down on a flat surface. Use a pocket hole jig to add pocket holes every 6 or so inches along the boards. Attach them together using pocket screws that are the appropriate size for your wood. If you are using reclaimed wood that is 1" thick, use 1½" screws; if you are using wood that is ¾" thick, use 1¼" pocket screws.

14. Cut the remaining 4" x 4" board to 44" long to act as the support between the two legs.

15. Place the table top upside down on the floor. Set the legs in place on top of the upside-down tabletop. Make sure the legs are centered across the planks and are an equal distance from each end of the tabletop. Lay the 4" x 4" support you cut in step 14 between the two legs to act as a spacer. Use wood glue to attach the legs to the tabletop. Predrill holes through the legs and screw the legs to the top using 2" screws.

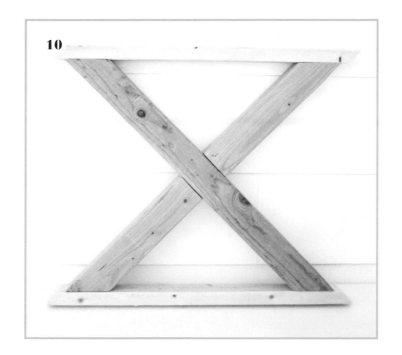

16. Drill two pocket holes on the underside of the 4" x 4" support piece.

17. Have a helper hold the support in place and add wood glue to each end. Use 2½" pocket screws to attach it to each X leg.

18. Add the stain and sealer of your choice. This table is finished using Rustoleum Kona Stain and General Finishes High Performance Topcoat in Flat. In general, when you are making any piece of furniture with rustic lumber or reclaimed wood, a flatter finish looks much better than a shiny one.

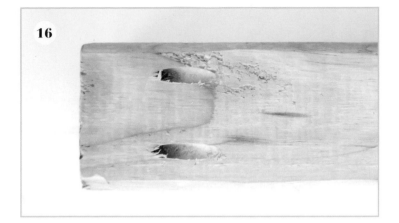

Epilogue

You Can Do This!

If you take nothing else from this book, know without a doubt that you, too, can turn ordinary wood planks into something truly beautiful for your home. Whether you have years of woodworking experience or are picking up a saw for the first time, I hope you feel inspired to go out and create something new.

As you create the projects here, feel free to put your own creative spin on them. Try a new paint finish, use a different type of wood, or come up with something completely different. But whatever you do, never stop creating.